LIFE IN 5D

A New Vision of Discipleship

Featuring the Discipleship Dynamics Assessment™

Charlie Self
Johan Mostert
Jamé Bolds

Foreword by Tom Nelson

Empowered Books
An imprint of ORU Press

Life in 5D

ISBN: 978-1-950971-33-6

5D Press is an imprint of BronzeBow Publishing.

Co-published with Empowered Books, an imprint of Oral Roberts University Press

© 2022 Discipleship Dynamics, LLC.

All rights reserved. Portions of this book may be quoted for review purposes. Use of more than 250 words must be secured with permission from the authors. No portions of this work may be reproduced or republished by any persons other than the authors without written permission from the authors.

All Scriptures are from the New International Version (2012) unless otherwise noted.

Discipleship Dynamics™ and the Discipleship Dynamics Assessment™ and DDA™ are protected resources of Discipleship Dynamics, LLC. and are used with permission.

Cover and Interior Design: David Koechel, Create Design Publish, Minneapolis MN

DEDICATIONS AND ACKNOWLEDGMENTS

We want to thank our patient family members, congregants, friends over the decades, and the hundreds of leaders who helped make this vision possible.

We are grateful for Dr. Lois Olena's skillful copy editing, the team at BronzeBow Publishing, and the many readers for their inputs. The wisdom in this book represents hundreds of thinkers, and thousands of assessment-takers. Any errors belong exclusively to the authors.

ENDORSEMENTS

Life in 5-D is a valiant attempt at regaining lost ground in the Church. If we are truly going to develop effective disciples of Jesus Christ, we will have to take seriously this book's proposals. More than another educational theory, it is well-researched tool for moving beyond mere knowledge of our faith to a mature representation of Jesus in every aspect of our lives. Those *Five Dimensions* give visibility to the abundant life in Christ as they become doorways revealing the fullest picture of what it means to be reconciled to God.

Byron D Klaus, President (1999-2015)
Assemblies of God Theological Seminary

While there is much in print about discipleship, I found *Life in 5-D* genuinely a new vision in discipleship. It is a carefully crafted study of "refining measurable outcomes of a disciple's life" with dimensional implication. Self, Mostert, and Bolds guide inspirational analysis and resolution with research-focused and a practical model for transformation. Their biblically rooted methodology bids a refreshing steadiness of comprehensive script and decidedly engaging, readable storyline. This is a gift to the church!

Joseph S. Girdler, D.Min., Crestwood, Kentucky
Superintendent ~ Kentucky Assemblies of God, 2004-present.

Life in 5-D provides a needed and helpful reimagining of discipleship. The five dimensions provide a framework of wholistic integration focused on the Spirit's work of making disciples more like Jesus. This approach utilizes a process rather than a class or event-driven model that all leaders and ages can apply to their context.

Steve Pulis, Ph.D.
Vice President Hope Education Network
Convoy of Hope

Endorsements

"As Christ followers, we are called to make disciples…but the question is often…how? Dr. Mostert is a gifted educator who brings passion, vision, and concepts that produce measurable outcomes for ministry! I feel so excited about how this book will impact my church and others in this critical season of the church."

Dr. Bob Griffith
Lead Pastor, Christ Chapel / Woodbridge, VA

"Discipleship, for all of life, is by and large quite broken. Discipleship has been compartmentalized at best…or worst? Thankfully, our brothers, Drs. Self and Mostert and soon-to-be, Dr. Bolds are timely with this resource to reboot our broken discipleship models and practices, so the church produces all-of-life disciples."

Luke Brad Bobo
Chief Program Officer, Arrabon and
Visiting Professor of Contemporary Culture,
Covenant Theological Seminary

"Western Christianity is facing a crisis of authentic benchmarks. Our spiritual compass is spinning like fan blades as true north is constantly being redefined by new trends and temporary movements. Life in 5-D is an invitation to stop the madness and do a hard reset of biblical standards that restore life, health, and balance."

Gene Roncone
Superintendent, Rocky Mountain Ministry Network of the
Assemblies of God

"*Life in 5-D* is a look at discipleship with a special focus on where we spend most of our productive week—what we do Monday through Friday. This integration of faith and work is often missing in our reflection about our walk and faith. So, this book not only causes us to reflect on what goes into discipleship but what that looks like in settings we usually do not think about when thinking about our spiritual growth and maturity before God."

Darrell Bock
Executive Director of Cultural Engagement, The Hendricks Center and Senior Research Professor of New Testament Studies, Dallas Theological Seminary / Dallas, Texas

"Discipleship is a primary responsibility of the Church. On that everyone agrees. What exactly does discipleship look like? Historically, the answers have been all over the map, always falling short of adequately defining this crucial function of the Church. Enter *Life in 5-D*. This outstanding book is a rigorously researched, biblically sound, and practitioner-validated resource that provides a clear and compelling description of discipleship paired with a reliable tool for measuring discipleship progress. *Life in 5-D* is helpful in any church context; leaders of mega- and micro-churches and every kind of church in between will find it an invaluable resource for cultivating a culture of discipleship in their faith community. I look forward to sharing this resource with the leaders we assist through Urban Islands Project and the Next Wave Community."

Steve Pike
President, Urban Islands Project
Founder, Next Wave Community

Endorsements

"What does it mean to be a disciple of Jesus? At one level, the answer is simple—learn to obey everything Jesus commanded and modeled, in reliance on the Holy Spirit. And yet, we sometimes sense we have lost our way, with too much attention on programs and not enough attention on pursuing outcomes that align with the way of Jesus. *Life in 5-D* offers a much-needed correction, calling us back to a clear vision of the goal—being transformed into the likeness of Christ in every dimension of our lives."

Matt Rusten
Executive Director, Made to Flourish

"The *ekklesia* has needed tools like this for centuries. Now it's here—for such a time as this, when the twenty-first century global Church is yearning for clarity toward fulfilling the Great Commission and realizing the End Game (Matt 28:18-20; 24:14)."

Chris Beard
Lead Pastor, Peoples Church Cincinnati
https://PeoplesChurch.co
Author of *Remarkable* https://remarkablethebook.com

"We have known Dr. Johan Mostert and Dr. Charlie Self for many years. In all the time we have known them, their passion and commitment to making disciples has never waned nor faded. This book reflects that passion. It is well structured, immensely helpful as a resource but, more importantly, they have written with passion and purpose. We highly recommend this useful book—not as "just another book for the bookshelf" but as a book that, if read and implemented, will produce life change and the extension of God's Kingdom."

Paul R. Alexander, PhD
President, Trinity Bible College and Graduate School
President, Assemblies of God Alliance for Higher Education
Chair, World Alliance for Pentecostal Theological Education

Carol Alexander, PhD
Dean, Graduate School at Trinity Bible College
and Graduate School

"*Life in 5-D* presents a holistic model for discipleship that reflects the Kingdom values of Jesus. As believers grow in intimacy with Christ, Scripture teaches that we will experience transformation spiritually, emotionally, and relationally but also move into the world with a sense of Kingdom clarity related to our work, callings, and finances. At the University of Northwestern–St. Paul, we use the authors' Discipleship Dynamics Assessment in our core curriculum because we want to send out graduates who are fully devoted to Jesus and who live out the values of Jesus wherever God sends them. *Life in 5-D* complements this assessment by offering a biblical and practical discussion of thirty-five holistic outcomes that we can expect to see in the life of a disciple."

Dale L. Lemke, PhD
Associate Professor of Christian Ministries,
University of Northwestern–St. Paul

"Bravo to the authors (Drs. Charlie Self and Johan Mostert, and Jamé Bolds) of the new book, *Life in 5-D: A New Vision of Discipleship!* This excellent tool will serve well alongside the Discipleship Dynamics Assessment tool they also crafted. This book focuses on outcomes for discipleship and is filled with narratives that give 'flesh to the bones' of the text. Its easy-to-read style makes it attractive for all those committed to the necessity of authentic discipleship. I loved reading it and strongly recommend that every church leader read it and pass it on!"

Dr. G. Robert Cook Jr.
Director of Senior Adult Ministries, Assemblies of God
Church Relations Director, Mercy Ships

Endorsements

"*Life in 5-D* draws on thirty-five measurable outcomes to offer Christians a resource-packed, carefully organized, and thoughtfully integrated five-dimensional plan toward mature discipleship grounded in love for God evident in spiritual practices (Spiritual Formation) and incorporating emotional health (Personal Wholeness), love for others (Healthy Relationships), purposeful work (Vocational Clarity), and daily life tasks (Economics and Work). Congratulations to the authors—*Life in 5-D* is a ministry."

Geoffrey W. Sutton, PhD
(https://suttong.com)
Psychologist and author of the highly recommended
Counseling and Psychotherapy with Pentecostal and Charismatic Christians

"Discipleship is so central and basic in the construct of the New Testament Church that it must serve as a core value and focus of ministry. The making of disciples was not a mere suggestion of Jesus, but His last and Great Commission before He ascended.

Regretfully, after the Early Church era, the Church through the ages has mostly lost this focus. Thankfully this is changing. In what I consider one of the most important restorations in the history of the Church, a global resurgence of this important truth has taken place over the last couple of years.

While there is a spontaneous, Holy Spirit-awakened realization of the importance of disciple-making, a clear need exists for guidance and equipment of believers and pastors alike. Perhaps the most comprehensive, responsible, and helpful tool known to me in this regard is the excellent and applicable Discipleship Assessment by Dr. Johan Mostert. The result of years of research and practical experience, it perhaps serves as the most effective instrument for both members and pastors to assess their level of growth as disciples of Christ.

What I particularly appreciate about the work has to do with the comprehensive approach to discipleship that includes not merely our so-called spiritual life, but, as it is supposed to be, the whole person in all dimensions of life. The life of a true disciple of Christ should not fragment into 'spiritual' and 'non-spiritual' departments. Every aspect of our lives should portray the Lordship and character of Christ.

I have known Johan for more than forty years and have the greatest appreciation for his consistent Christian walk, his practical experience in ministry, and his academic achievements. This product results from extensive study and research on the subject of discipleship assessment and guidance.

As this book will greatly empower pastors to minister in a relevant way in the twenty-first century, I recommend this ministry tool with the certainty that it will provide much required assistance to those in ministry.

Dr. Isak Burger
Former President, Apostolic Faith Mission of South Africa
Author of *The Fire Falls in Africa* and other titles in Afrikaans

"Dr.Charles Self stands out as and individual whoq has redefined an entire era by nurturing and developing catalytic lleaders. In his capable hands, intelliect and faith, culture and grace, humanity and history seamlessly merge. He and his co-authors offer a transformative vision and the tools needed for discipleship to touch all of life."

Rev. Dr. Roger Valci
Pastor and strategist
Founder / President of City Serve *Orlando*

"Jamé Bolds' chapters on faith, work, and economics are gold. The call of Christ to make disciples is made a reality not only within the church walls but in the workplace! These truly golden insights can help build the Church."

Alan Kelso
President/CEO, Living Water Communities LLC

Endorsements

"Five (5), Thirty-Five (5), and One (1). You will remember those numbers as you and your congregation read, study, and implement the usable, practical wisdom in this book from three respected pastor theologians. Faithful discipleship engages five dimensions that will result in thirty-five outcomes with the aim of developing one integrated, holistic follower/community of Jesus Christ. When life and faith and congregational ministry often fragment, segment, and get siloed, this book reminds us that the living God desires the whole—all our heart, soul, mind, and strength—the entirety of who we are, the entirety of creation, and the fullness of what God has created us to be. This book and its authors aim for that. They walk with you in the gentle and prophetic way that only an experienced loving pastor who has combed the depths of the soul and traversed the crucible of congregational life can. *Life in 5-D* is a must-buy, must-read, must-do."

Rev. Neal D. Presa, PhD
New Brunswick Theological Seminary
www.nealpresa.com

"What happens when you get public intellectual, a community psychologist, and an economic theologian to write a book? The outcome is a brilliant whole life discipleship path that measures discipleship in every area of life. Get this book and memorize it."

Stephen D. Lentz, Esq.
Partner/Senior Counsel, Anchor Legal Group, PLLC

"Jamé Bolds and his co-authors show us in this book how disciples are made at work and not necessarily at church. The chapter on faith, work, and economics is gold."

Bishop Clifton R. Clarke, PhD
Senior Pastor, New Beginnings Church, Simi Valley, CA
Bishop of San Fernando Valley, CA (Church of God, Cleveland)
Visiting Professor, Oral Roberts University, Tulsa OK

"I believe with all my heart that there is no such thing as secular employment for the believer. The question is not, 'Are you in ministry?' The question is, 'Who pays you to do ministry?' For some, it is the church. For most, it is the marketplace. Unfortunately, we spend a majority of our time in discipleship preparing people for their hour of serving in the church rather than discipling them on how to use their gift five days a week in all callings to the marketplace. Learning how to see how faith, work, and economics as a starting place for discipleship is a gift that Jamé Bolds and his co-authors are giving to the church. I highly recommend this book. It will change your philosophy on discipleship. It will change your church. And it will change our communities!"

Douglas Witherup, MTh, D.Min.
Senior Pastor, Multiply Family of Churches
Professor and Author

FOREWORD

In his inspired first-century letter to the church at Colossae, the Apostle Paul provides a guiding framework for Christian calling and the mission of discipleship, writing: "We proclaim Him, admonishing everyone, teaching everyone with all wisdom that we may present everyone mature in Christ" (Col 1:28) As apprentices of Jesus, a growing spiritual maturity and an increasing Christlikeness of life should be our life's primary aim. But what does the path of discipleship look like, and how do we know whether we are making good progress on the road to spiritual maturity? How might we better assess the fruitfulness of our journey of faith?

From a deep reservoir of theological reflection and many years of practical experience, the authors of *Life in 5-D* have designed innovative and helpful tools for assessing the disciple's progress toward maturity. In doing so, they have made a significant and timely contribution to the church's discipleship mission. By casting a compelling vision of whole life discipleship, they gracefully challenge impoverished views of discipleship speaking only to the smallest privatized parts of a disciple's daily life.

The authors raise a crucial question, "What does a disciple look like on Tuesday at 10 a.m. anywhere but the church?" This question looks not merely for the parameters of authentic belief but also for the very down-to-earth, observable, and demonstrable evidences or outcomes of authentic belief in all dimensions of human life. Walking in step with the Early Church, they place a most needed focus on what some refer to as the *habitus* of Christian discipleship—those distinct, often counter cultural attitudes, behaviors, practices, and manners of apprentices of Jesus informed by Christian faith in every nook and cranny of daily life. Both paradigmatically as well as practically, *Life in 5-D* wonderfully narrows the all too common and perilous Sunday to Monday gap.

I feel truly encouraged and excited about this book, for I believe it will not only bring Jesus great glory but also make the bride of Christ more beautiful as apprentices of Jesus make greater progress in that joyful, yet long obedience in the same direction.

Tom Nelson
Lead Senior Pastor, Christ Community Church, Kansas City, KS
Founder and President, Made to Flourish
Author: *Work Matters, The Economics of Neighborly Love, and The Flourishing Pastor*

TABLE OF CONTENTS

Dedication and Acknowledgments 3

Endorsements. . . . .

Foreword by Tom Nelson 4

Preface: Facing Reality: Time for Hope
and Measurement 17

Introduction: Come Join the Revolution—
From Programs to Outcomes 31

Dimension One: Loving God with
All Our Being (Spiritual Formation) 47

Dimension Two: Letting God Liberate Us from
the Inside Out (Personal Wholeness) 73

Dimension Three: Loving Our Neighbor
Every Day (Healthy Relationships) 101

Dimension Four: Walking in the Good Works God
Has Designed for Us (Vocational Clarity) 117

Dimension Five: Offering All of Daily Life as
Worship (Economics and Work) 135

Conclusion: The Path Forward: Envision,
Equip, and Assess. 153

Afterword by Scott Hagan 157

Resources 179

Select Bibliography. 190

PREFACE:
Facing Reality:
Time for Hope and Measurement!

The world has changed.

One of the changes leaders face today has to do with the nature of disciplemaking. As one local pastor expressed in 2021, "I have a wonderful church, and we are by all measures a success. Baptisms are up, giving is solid, and new ministries are being developed. Yet I have an uneasy feeling that we are not really making disciples."

Steve Pike, founder of Urban Islands Mission and Next Wave Community, speaking to church planters in 2020, offers insights for the road ahead: "What was the norm for church planting and revitalization in the twentieth century will not work for the twenty-first century. We need nothing less than a reimagination of the local church and her mission, with disciple-making as the focus."

Lisa Slayton, founder of Tamim partners and an expert in executive coaching and organizational strategies, said to a group of leaders in 2021, "We are in an unprecedented moment of upheaval and disruption. Character and openness to new paradigms will be essential if organizations are going to thrive."

Julie and her husband, Rob, along with their two teenagers, have served as faithful members of their church for ten years. The COVID-19 pandemic took a toll on them. Working and learning from home isolated them from their extended family, church community, friends, and co-workers. They did watch their church's Sunday service online and used the outlines provided for some conversations, but it was not the same.

They were vaccinated and boosted, and sought to comply with all the local restrictions. Over time, they found themselves angry, irritated, and less patient with each other and others. They missed their small group and youth group. After full days of being online, they did not want to be on a screen for their spiritual life. Their gym was restrictive, and they found it difficult exercising with a mask. They did walk a bit but found themselves snacking more and gaining some unwanted pounds.

Additionally, the pandemic unearthed some emotional issues for both Julie and Rob. They loved each other and did not seriously wound each other, but old extended-family tensions, childhood and adolescent events, and work frustrations all came to the surface with new intensity. They realized that their church activities and busy lives served as a cover for serious emotional and relational needs.

Cultural and political conflicts on social media only added to these personal challenges. Lifetime friends unfriended them. Family members got angry when they did not repeat the same political slogans.

They called their pastor and in frustration asked, "What does God expect of us?" The pastor listened, empathized, and then asked if they were praying, reading their Bibles, and continuing to give and volunteer where they could. They tried not to yell and said, "Yes! We are doing all that… but why are all these feelings hitting us now? How is God working in this moment?"

Julie and Rob's discipleship challenges are felt by millions of faithful Christians. The pandemic did create some tensions, but what it really did was bring a variety of issues to the surface that were never a part of their "normal" church life.

Our Challenge

Everywhere we turn, pastors, spiritual leaders, and thoughtful Christians of all traditions are lamenting the challenges of discipleship. The pandemic and other sea changes in culture are compelling leaders to reflect and reimagine ministry. Consider these realities:

- We have never had more resources for spiritual growth…yet many believers are emaciated, with no clear picture of what spiritual health looks like.
- Leaders find it difficult to imagine spiritual health, too, when so much time is spent doing emotional, relational, and economic triage.
- Leaders feel frustrated, and the number leaving pastoral ministry grows daily. The emotional, mental, financial, and social stresses are real.
- Millions are deciding that their experience of church can consist only of watching an online service at home.

- An increasing number of Christians now decline to state either a tradition or an affiliation with a particular movement.

- A large percentage of spiritual leaders get all of their preaching and teaching material from the Internet and simply refine and repackage it for their audiences. Sometimes this works, but the actual maturation and sanctification of the people of God remains woefully lacking.

- Spiritual leaders face cultures that are at best apathetic and at worst hostile to Christian faith and values.

- Economic and social changes are accelerating. Preparing women and men for the new world of work ahead is an imperative, not an option.

- Ideological and political polarization is harming church communities and cooperation in mission. Jesus prayed for and is the source of unity among Christians, but a new vision of discipleship and mission is needed to repair the wounds of generations.

- Historical injustices are front and center, and it will require maturity among thoughtful believers to heal, restore, give hope, and renew communities.

Back to Julie and Rob. What is their picture of wholeness in Christ, from their own health to the health of their neighborhood and nation? They love God and their kids, and they want to be faithful to their church and see people come to Jesus; however, they do not have an adequate vision of God's Kingdom that can sustain them in our troubled world.

No More Status Quo!

This book is about a revolution in discipleship (and by extension, mission) that focuses on biblical outcomes that touch all dimensions of human experience. These outcomes are measurable! The authors have created the most complete assessment of whole-life discipleship ever offered. It can be found here: www.discipleshipdynamics.com. We take the guesswork out of whether a person or community is making progress!

Without lapsing into legalism, there must be a better way forward for God's people so they can love in deed as well as declaration, connect Sunday's ecstasies with Monday's ethics, and find true healing and hope from the inside out.

So, What Do We Do?

All three of this book's authors have decades of experience serving the local and global church and the broader community; leading organizations; and wrestling with emotional, economic, institutional, and social challenges. Before we answer the question of what we should do, here is a bit of our background. We love the church and her mission to "make disciples" (Matt 28:19).

Meet the Authors

Dr. Charlie Self

I have had the honor of over forty years of service to the local and global church, educational communities, businesses, and non-profits that care for the common good. Being a public intellectual, I enjoy collecting and offering insights on current challenges.

For over thirty years I have been learning and writing about whole-life discipleship and the inseparability of discipleship and mission. For the last decade, I have served a variety of networks promoting the integration of faith, work, and economic wisdom for pastors, educators, local churches, and parachurch missions. (See these organizations in our Resources section at the end of the book.)

With Dr. Johan Mostert and Rev. Jamé Bolds, I have worked tirelessly to offer a comprehensive (not exhaustive) vision of wholeness in Christ. The fruit of this labor is the unique Discipleship Dynamics Assessment ™. When we see the wholeness Christ offers and have a clear picture of our strengths and weaknesses, progress is possible.

In my travels and trainings across the U.S. and in Europe, the need for clarity, completeness, and measurability in discipleship proved evident. Almost a decade ago, I asked a discipleship pastor of a megachurch how things were going. He smiled and answered, "We have almost 80 percent of our members in small groups!" I rejoiced with him for this unusually high participation rate and commended his organizational and motivational gifts. Then I asked, "And how do you know if people are growing? Even more, how do the participants themselves know they are making progress?" He looked at me and said, "Testimonies." I then asked, "What vision of wholeness does everyone have?" He reviewed a good, simple mission statement. We parted, and I went away determined to help others paint a picture of maturity even more clearly. My friend's answers were sound but felt incomplete.

I am always hopeful and praying earnestly for a local and global awakening that will connect Sunday's joy with Monday's justice, i.e., Sunday's worship with Monday's work. I believe that the vision and wisdom of *Life in 5D* can serve as a small part of this beautiful foretaste of God's Kingdom.

Dr. Johan Mostert

After five years of pastoral ministry in South Africa, God made it clear to me that I was missing a critical leg on my theoretical three-legged stool. I loved the Lord; that was a firm foundation from the time of my youth. Though well-trained in the Scriptures and with the ability to engage in all manner of apologetic discussions and debates, I still had a fractured understanding of the persons I was called to serve—i.e., the objects of my pastoral ministry. I concluded that no pastor can succeed in his or her task of promoting the Kingdom agenda with one of these three elements missing! We were tasked to equip the saints for the work of the ministry (Eph 4:11-12), but I was confronted by teenage pregnancies, family violence, and broken marriages. I felt perplexed at the behavior of elders incapable of managing their anger or treating newcomers to our fellowship with respect. My people loved to participate in Sunday worship but struggled with anxiety and depression and treated their domestic workers with disdain. My people group (Afrikaners) were a God-fearing tribe who constructed a society that was outwardly religious but struggled with the realities of their racial prejudices and apartheid practices. The church there generally dismissed the AIDS crisis as a failure of personal holiness rather than an opportunity to serve vulnerable individuals.

I engaged in multiple years of graduate study in the social sciences and obtained certifications as a psychologist and social worker in an attempt to redress the traditional concept of discipleship. The Scriptures have such rich insights into life beyond spiritual disciplines to include the "weightier elements of the law" (Matt 23:23): justice, mercy, and faith. My studies opened opportunities for me to serve the Church in South Africa as Director of Social Welfare where we administered ten homes for the aged, pioneered family-style cottage homes for 220 children, managed a team of social workers in seven offices throughout the nation, initiated international adoption services, and coordinated the activities of hundreds of faith-based community associations attached to local churches.

In 2004, I emigrated to the United States to serve as Professor of Community Psychology at the Assemblies of God Theological Seminary (AGTS), where we trained Licensed

Professional Counselors to function as mental health professionals comfortable providing professional services in a theologically integrated manner. In this capacity I have led trainings in Costa Rica, Israel, Canada, Swaziland, Mozambique, Malawi, Kenya, Nigeria, and Singapore.

In 2016, I was privileged to return to the field of social work practice and took up a position with AG Family Services (dba COMPACT Family Services) to spearhead an evidence-based intervention to assist local churches to increase the quality of foster care.

Rev. Jamé Bolds

I am Charlie and Johan's junior colleague, collaborator, money mover, business brain, and PhD chaser. I am raising a family and active in pastoral ministry. Before leading church revitalizations, I began my professional life at the Acton Institute where we studied how churches and nonprofits address issues of poverty and economic development. This lit a fire in my heart to learn and apply the practical application of how money works for a ministry multiplier. Over the years, our denomination has asked my wife and I to revitalize various churches in New Jersey and Virginia. Jennifer's training and experience as a professional counselor and corporate consultant focused on emotional intelligence have proven invaluable in serving others.

At our current church, we are living a miracle. The structure of the church was dated; the bylaws had not been updated since Acts 2 (smile) and the building since the early 2000s. The church was in debt over $1M. They were running a structural deficit, so servicing the debt was almost impossible; they also had a preschool with a fiscally-unhealthy burn rate. We were running about fifty people on Sundays. From what I could tell, based on limited data and early financial modeling, the church was about sixty days away from closing. With all this, on a warm spring day, twenty-eight people elected us to serve as their pastors.

I feel grateful and humbled by the goodness of God to lead Victory Church (Yorktown, VA) in a five-year, $4.5M revitalization. At the ten-year mark, Victory will be an over $30M turnaround with forty-six acres in two counties, two 501(c)(3) nonprofits, a premier preschool, a one-hundred-unit retirement community, several LLCs, four economic engines, and two buildings—all debt-free.

I consult with churches and nonprofits to structure them so they never run out of money. I have built philanthropic foundations. I even ran a U.S. Congressional campaign. I teach as an adjunct professor for Gordon-Conwell Theological Seminary. I hold graduate degrees in theology and economics, and I am a Ph.D. candidate at Universiteit Stellenbosch, SA.

In the language of Nimi Wariboko, I consider myself an economic theologian, as applied to a branch of practical theology that "Aspires to show how theological categories are useful and understanding economic and interpreting economies. I also work to clarify how economic concepts and reasoning can be employed to enrich ethical constructions."[1] These categories remain of great importance when we think about the interplay and competing claims of both theology and economics as they relate to building disciples.

As pastors, we do not simply disciple people to be good church people on Sunday. We must disciple them to function as Kingdom contributors on Monday. Most people spend more time at work than at any other daily activity. This is why I am part of the Discipleship Dynamics Assessment™ team: we share a vision to shape disciples in all facets of life.

In my pastoral life and consulting work, I have seen firsthand two jagged little pills to swallow when we talk about whole-life discipleship: (1) addressing the Sunday-Monday heresy, and (2) outcomes, not just outputs/programs. The Sunday-Monday heresy takes place when Christians see their faith as private and not public—a way of practicing worship in church but not in the community. This heresy entails faith concerned with justification but not justice, seeing salvation as only personal but not impacting the community. The second 'pill to swallow' when it comes to whole-life discipleship involves the need to focus on outcomes rather than on outputs/programs. Outcomes means focusing on the question, "What does a disciple look like on Tuesday at 10 a.m. anywhere but at the church?" Is discipleship taking root in that person's spiritual formation, healthy relationships, personal wholeness, vocational

---

[1] Nimi Wariboko, *Economics in Spirit and Truth: A Moral Philosophy of Finance* (Basingstoke: Springer, 2014), 14.

clarity, and of course in their work and economic wisdom? Outputs are simply the programs that churches offer, but outcomes are what our churches and Christian organizations produce. At Victory Church, we call our people "Victors." I feel consumed with the notion, "What is a Victor?"

I began this journey as a student at a prestigious evangelical seminary and liberal divinity school. Later, I earned another graduate degree at a prestigious university, studying the practice of management and economics. Today, I am completing a Ph.D. to put it all together. I started this journey at a think tank, then moved to the local church, then to the academy, and now I've moved back to local church. All of this is in pursuit of *Life in 5-D*, disciples following Jesus in all dimensions of life and having an impact in all domains of our world.

As a pastor, I urge you to take this book to your leadership teams, your staff, and your congregants. Read it, think about it, digest it, pray about it, and wrestle with it. This book represents our collaboration, including countless hours of listening to leaders, doing survey research, compiling statistics, flying coast to coast, and discovering many eye-opening findings. Years of research is our commitment to you—we have given you a roadmap of making healthy disciples. Once you have your survey done and you see your dashboard, read over the "how to" guides on the website, and reach out to us. We want to help you make disciples.

O.K., So What Do We Do?

We aspire to revolutionize discipleship. *Revolutions begin with reimagination.* Merely tweaking current ideas and structures, even significant reformation, will not produce the desired changes desperately needed. Here is the revolution in one sentence:

Discipleship is the Spirit-empowered process of aligning programs and activities to reflect biblical outcomes that will allow the Spirit to produce believers who display the character of Christ in all dimensions of their lives.

Disciples must have a vision of wholeness in Christ that touches all dimensions of life and be able to measure their progress.

Hebrews 13:7 encourages believers to follow their leaders and "consider the outcome of their way of life and imitate their faith."[2] This verse is followed by the affirmation, "Jesus Christ is the same yesterday and today and forever" (v. 8). Put simply, wholeness in Christ is not obscure or relegated to a few super saints. The outcomes of growing disciples are biblical, universal (fitting all classes and cultural contexts), and doable with help of the Holy Spirit.

We invite all thoughtful believers—especially those who care for others—to join our journey and accept the challenge. We can do better!

---

2 All Scriptures are from the New International Version (2012) unless otherwise noted.

For Reflection

1. What challenges do you face in your own spiritual growth?

2. In addition to the Bible and your pastor's sermons, what experiences and resources have helped your Christian growth?

3. Who are the people who most influence your walk with the Lord?

INTRODUCTION:

Come Join the Revolution—From Programs to Outcomes

"We must adventure or die."[3]

"What are you aiming for, Charlie? You can scatter your shots about, hoping to hit a target, or focus and hit the bullseye. The Holy Spirit can help you focus."[4]

"Leaders articulate what 'there' looks like and help their community follow Christ to that destination."[5]

Thank you for staying with us! We want to introduce the Five Dimensions and help you begin a fresh pathway of love and service to our Lord. The five chapters that follow will offer more detail on each dimension. Our Resources section at the end will give more detail about the Discipleship Dynamics Assessment designed as a tool for measuring progress in individuals and groups. We hope its breadth

---

[3] Tod Bolsinger, *Canoeing the Mountains: Christian Leadership in Uncharted Territory* (Downers Grove: IVP, 2015), 24.

[4] Os Guinness, personal conversation with Charlie Self, 1987.

[5] Johan Mostert, presentation at the Assemblies of God theological Seminary, January 30, 2013.

and depth will inspire leaders' imaginations as they equip others, and individual Christians' growth in grace.

Back to Julie and Rob

Everything we share in this book must impact regular people on Tuesday afternoon! Our reimagining of discipleship applies to all believers of all cultures, traditions, and ages. In the words attributed to Gregory the Great, what we present must be, "Broad and deep, shallow enough here for the Lamb to go wading, but deep enough there for the elephant to swim."[6]

As we take this journey together, let's keep our own needs and those of Julie and Rob in mind.

Selah: A Pause for Theology!

We appreciate tradition distinctives, but this book and the DDA were designed for the broadest possible Christian audience. As we share in this book, we are assuming the following beliefs that are embraced by global Christians:

- We love the Bible and believe it is divinely inspired and the final authority for faith and practice.

- We affirm the Nicene Creed of 381, affirming the deity and humanity of Jesus, the beauty of

---

6 Gregory the Great (fl. 600 AD), *Moralia in Job*, book 4 (also attributed to Origen and Augustine) Grateful to the Dead, accessed June 29, 2022, https://gratefultothedead.com/2010/02/26/quote-of-the-day-scripture-is-like-a-river-broad-and-deep-shallow-enough-here-for-the-lamb-to-go-wading-but-deep-enough-there-for-the-elephant-to-swim/.

the Trinity, and the historical faith, "once for all entrusted to the saints."

- The local church is central to God's mission, and—when possible—all believers are part of a concrete, local community of faith.

- God's mission embraces the whole person and the whole world; all Christians are invited to join as co-laborers in this ministry of reconciliation and restoration.

- God's community is hospitable and holy, welcoming all people of every background and culture, calling them to a life shaped by the Cross and resurrection of Jesus Christ, evident by faith, hope, and love.

- Discipleship and mission are inseparable. Methods will vary, and people will employ different experiences and processes, but the aim is always presenting every believer mature in Christ.

- We are centered in the gospel of Christ and refuse to let our faith be held captive to human ideologies, political extremes, or ethnic and national divisions.

O.K., Back to Life in 5-D!

Our starting point was a simple question: "What does a healthy disciple look like?" Another way of saying this is, "What are the outcomes of a Christ-centered life under the kingdom of God?" One leader was blunt: "What does life look like when Christ is Lord of all?"

The Bible itself contains several summaries of what God expects of His followers. In the Old Testament, The Ten Commandments (Exod 20 and Deut 5) are imperatives for the people of God, outlining a life of gratitude rooted in God's election, deliverance, and covenant-love (Exod 4-20). Micah 6:8, in poetic fashion, summarizes a whole-life commitment of justice, mercy, and devotion.

Jesus shared the foundational attributes of Kingdom life in the Beatitudes (Matt 5) and His blessings (Luke 6) from the sermons on the mount and plain. Jesus told His followers that the commands to love God with one's whole being and love one's neighbor as oneself are the foundation and fruit of all of God's ways (Matt 22:37-40).

Paul the Apostle, in the great love chapter of 1 Corinthians 13, unveils attitudes and actions that are the fruit of a life devoted to Christ. The fruit of the Spirit and the virtues of divine life are outlined in Galatians 5:22-23. Peter offers another list of beautiful virtues in 2 Peter 1:1-10.

"O.K., we get it...so how is *Life in 5-D* any different from what we know?

Glad you asked! Here is the BIG IDEA:

Life is dimensional. Following Jesus means welcoming the Holy Spirit into every facet of human experience.

We began with the implications of the Great Commandment of Jesus:

- Loving God with all our being: this is **spiritual formation** and all the classic spiritual disciplines are integrated here (Matt 22:37-40).

- Loving our neighbor: **healthy relationships** remain critical to the Kingdom. In fact, the Apostle John says that one cannot claim to love God and hate one's brother (1 John 2-4).

- Loving oneself: **personal wholeness** is in view here. The Bible assumes reasonable self-care and makes no distinction between spiritual and emotional maturity (Eph 4:22-5:1).

As we explored our reflections and listened to many leading voices, an important fourth dimension appeared: a sense of personal purpose or calling that we titled **vocational clarity**. We are all more than our current jobs or titles, and God has general and specific good works for each believer (Rom 12:4-8; Eph 2:8-10; 4:1-16).

This decade of research coincided with all of us serving as leaders in a wonderful upsurge of interest in the integration of faith and work, eliminating the "Sunday vs. Monday heresy" (Jamé) and honoring all domains of work as part of God's mission. But more than simplistic work ethics exists here: Christians need to know how they contribute to the economies they are part of and that economic wisdom remains vital to flourishing personally and for the community.

Put simply, all the character transformation we speak of in the first four dimensions takes place as believers spend their days working. Now we have the fifth dimension: **economics and work**. Our Lord Jesus perfectly fulfilled the Father's plan in the dusty reality of daily work, laboring as an artisan until led to commence His public messianic ministry (Heb 2-4).

"O.K., wait a minute! You are going too far here. How does my day job that I hate relate at all to following Jesus, other than not cursing and being honest? My real spiritual work is when I help lead a Bible study and volunteer in the nursery. Don't try to spiritualize my job." These words were spoken by a spiritual leader in 2012 as Johan, Charlie, and Jamé hosted a listening event and welcomed input from spiritual leaders. The one who spoke so provocatively was a friend of ours and trying to get the discussion moving—and oh my, did the discussion get lively! A firestorm erupted when Charlie said that spiritual formation takes place as people do their daily work, not just in private moments of devotional practice.

So, in review, there are Five Dimensions of Life that must be considered in any whole-life vision of discipleship:

- **Spiritual Formation**: loving God with all our being. This is the foundation of the following four dimensions.

- **Personal Wholeness**: emotional health and maturity. These are inseparable for spiritual maturity and sanctification.

- **Healthy Relationships**: loving our neighbors. This includes all relationships being honoring to God.

- **Vocational Clarity**: understanding our God-given purpose. We are always more than just our current job description.

- **Economics and Work**: the daily task we do each day, interacting with the broader world. God's mission takes place as we do our work each day, and our work is more than just a means to an end!

As these dimensions came into focus, we also worked at refining the measurable outcomes of a disciple's life, since these dimensions are part of a seamless life of worship and work, being and doing, devotion and discipline before the Lord. Over time, what began with over one hundred outcomes were narrowed to forty (version 1), and today we have thirty-five (version 3); these refined, verified outcomes offer a comprehensive picture of wholeness in Christ.

Why Does All This Matter?

It is the task of spiritual leaders to make biblical truth applicable in everyday life. It is not enough to tell someone, "Be more like Jesus," "Live a surrendered life," or "Just trust and obey." These are good phrases, but they are incomplete. Believers need a clear picture, a vision of what all the messages, disciplines, and hard work is leading toward! We believe that seeing "Life in 5-D" and understanding the practical outcomes will help all believers grow. Doing so also will help spiritual leaders organize their programs and resources around a vision that captivates the imagination and calls upon the best efforts of all.

Once again, the focus of our book: *Discipleship is the Spirit-empowered process of aligning programs and activities to reflect biblical outcomes that will allow the Spirit to produce believers who display the character of Christ in all dimensions of their lives. Disciples must have a vision of wholeness in Christ that touches all dimensions of life and be able to measure their progress.*

A few years ago, a children's pastor at a church in California saw our work and said, "This is great! I can see my kids celebrating their faith. May I offer a sentence for each dimension? I am so excited to have all my kids and their families on the same page."

Here is his summary of "Life in 5-D" for kids:

- "I feel close to Jesus, and He hears my prayers." (Spiritual Formation)
- "I feel good about myself. God loves me." (Personal Wholeness)
- "I am getting along with my family and friends." (Healthy Relationships)
- "I know what I am good at." (Vocational Clarity)
- "I am doing my chores and homework for Jesus." (Economics and Work)

And here is a picture of what we will unpack in the following chapters:

Introduction

We envision millions of Christians committed to this vision, offering all of life as worship and willingly doing the work to mature in their faith and increase their influence for God's Kingdom. We also see thousands of leaders using the DDA as a vital tool calibrating their effectiveness.

Will you join the revolution of reimagining discipleship and mission that will prepare us for a coming awakening? Will you have the courage to take the DDA and lead your community into a new era of fruitfulness?

In the Resources section at the end, we have all kinds of practical guides for using the DDA in your context. *We challenge you to take the Assessment (*www.discipleshipdynamics.com*) right now, and then read the rest of this book to learn strategies for growth.*

The revolution in discipleship begins with a fresh vision of wholeness for both individuals and communities and a commitment from leaders and their communities to engage in the serious work that is needed.

Here is the key: All dimensions are connected! When we struggle with one or two outcomes, that affects six or seven others. For example, if we hold an unforgiving attitude toward a colleague at work, that disposition can influence our home life, our inner peace, and even our clarity of thinking about work details. And of course, Jesus says in Matthew 6 that our failure to forgive keeps us from enjoying God's forgiveness. One the other hand, when we make progress in one outcome, others improve. If we continually learn to hear God's voice, we will act more sensitively to others, function as a better teammate at work, and become a capable mentor of others.

Steve Garber, author of *A Seamless Life* and *Visions of Vocation*, challenges his listeners and readers to recover St. Benedict's call to an integrated life of *Ora et Labora* (prayer and work) as we heed God's calling to enjoy His presence and engage in working with God for the reconciliation and restoration of His creation. Romans 12:1-2 and Colossians 3:17-23 provide remarkable instruction for followers of Jesus, helping them to end 'religion as usual' by offering *all* of life as worship before God.

As we dive into each of the dimensions and outcomes, some hopeful realism is in order. The Five Dimensions are relatively easy to remember, but what about trying to keep all thirty-five outcomes in our heads? If you can, great. But most of us do not need a huge list of things to add to already busy lives!

Welcome the dimensions as a daily examination and then look at the outcomes weekly, noting growth or points of struggle. If you use the DDA, please invite a mature friend or leader to help you prioritize what the Lord is doing in your life and offer encouragement as you progress. I (Charlie) use the dimensions as questions *almost* (I have to be honest—life can get crazy!) daily:

Am I growing closer to the Holy Trinity, enjoying God, and welcoming His conviction and comfort?

Am I becoming more hopeful and whole inside, allowing God to liberate me from negative history and increase my vision for the future?

Are all my relationships doing well? Am I cultivating new friends while nurturing the lifelong ones?

Am I clearer on my personal calling and how it honors God and serves others?

Am I doing today's work well, even as I await future blessings?

Here is another insight that will make this whole book, and the vision we are presenting, come alive: *No dimension of life or domain of society is outside of the kingdom of God. Jesus Christ is King over all.* Of course, His Kingdom invitation is voluntary, not coercive. *Transformation of individuals and systems rests on the purposeful actions of God's people and providential activities of people of conscience.*

"I think I see what you are saying!" exclaimed a seminar participant in one of our listening events across the country. "Life is not a check list of priorities. It is Jesus growing in us and affecting every part of us!" We could not say it better!

Beyond the Personal

Just as Jesus cares about our five personal dimensions, He also cares about all facets of the creation. They all include economic, social, educational/intellectual, cultural, and political life. In one of our next books, we will offer wisdom about navigating these important social concerns in more detail. For now, it is essential that we make three connections.

Introduction

First, spiritual renewal must be joined with social change for sustainable awakening. Otherwise, our faith is merely privately engaging and publicly irrelevant. As we have already said twice, justification by faith must be joined with faithful justice (Mic 6:8; Rom 14:17).

Second, personal spiritual growth is always biblically connected to participation in the local church. We were baptized into Christ in the name of the Father, Son, and Holy Spirit—*and* we were baptized into the body of Christ (1 Cor 12:13). There is no place for "I love Jesus, but not the Church." First John 2-4 makes it clear that every believer is an organic part of the Body—global and local. Yes, one can be saved without official membership in a church; however, by God's design, we only flourish and fulfill our purpose in real, concrete community.

Third, all growth in maturity and mission depends on our surrender to the work of the Holy Spirit (Rom 8; 1 Cor 12-14). Our mind, affections, and will actively cooperate with the Bible and the inner work of grace the Spirit brings. We need divine help! Humility remains the vital precondition for divine favor and power.

As we enjoy this journey, the correspondence of the Apostle Paul with the Corinthians believers proves helpful. In 1 Corinthians, Paul's second letter to these believers, he tries to help this enthusiastic community grow up and realize that passion must unite with principles, and ecstatic experiences must align with sound theology and ethics. After 1 Corinthians, Paul writes another letter, urging better discipline and relationships. Then, Paul writes 2 Corinthians as his fourth letter to help the community move toward reconciliation. The Corinthians were immature, divided over their favorite apostle (1 Cor 1-4), compromising on sexual ethics (5-7), taking each other to a pagan secular court (5), contentious about matters of conscience (8-10), disorderly and unjust in their worship services (11-14), and even questioning basic doctrine (15)! Believers and churches in the twenty-first century face similar challenges and good discipleship will encourage personal maturity and community cohesion.

Over the course of decades of pastoral work, I (Charlie) have discovered that *believers can age without actually maturing. Chronology does not guarantee character*, and experiences without subsequent reflection and ethical refinement prove insufficient. I have seen many folks in their sixties and seventies with the emotional maturity of teenagers! It felt disheartening to see folks testify to experiences with the Lord at camp meetings but demonstrate little progress over the decades.

Friends, Let's Grow up and Stay Alert!

As we look more deeply into each dimension, discovering the that life the Lord intends for all of us, we must remain alert to the reality of intensifying spiritual warfare. Our adversary enjoys keeping believers apathetic, with low expectations and lukewarm passions. We may be headed to heaven, but our impact on earth for eternity will be limited if we passively accept the status quo and are not intentional in our growth. Here are three insights that will help us live as victors and not victims as we move forward:

One: Our life will include both joy and suffering, unexplainable difficulties, and unbelievable delights. We are always walking in both, "the power of his [Christ's] resurrection and participation in his sufferings" (Phil 3:10). When we embrace this paradoxical power of Christ, we will find greater endurance and discover fresh wisdom as we reflect on how God is at work for our good in all circumstances (Rom 8:15-39). For those of us who love theology, this is an integration of a theology of the Cross and a theology of glory.

Two: Satan has no weapon against humility. This is why both James and Peter exhort believers to humble themselves and then see the enemy flee as they resist his temptations (Jas 4; 1 Pet 5). When we aim for God's glory and the good of others, eschew power-seeking for service, and celebrate others more than ourselves, we are filled with peace, trusted with divine power, and fulfilling God's will in all we do (Mark 10:45).

Three: Expect an inner battle in addition to circumstantial challenges. As we embrace the 5 Dimensions and 35 Outcomes of our life in Christ, all kinds of distractions, distortions, and even depressing thoughts will fill our minds: "Nothing ever changes." "These ideas are fine for some people, but not for me." "This is too complex." "I am not important." In addition to these thoughts, we must also guard against spiritual pride as we embark on this journey.

With hearts full of faith, let's take a deep dive together into these dimensions.

For Reflection

1. How do you see God working in your daily life of work?

2. What are the most frustrating things about your current home and work life?

3. What aspects of your life do you need the Lord's help with right now?

Dimension One:

Loving God with All Our Being (Spiritual Formation)

"Does God really like me?
The biblical answer is a resounding, "Yes!"[7]

"Human sovereignty leads to frustration. Divine sovereignty leads all responsive persons to fulfillment."[8]

"If we can ever receive from a man an honest answer to the question, what comes into your mind when you think about God, we could with certainty predict the spiritual future of than man."[9]

"What we think about God is important. What God thinks about us is even more important."[10]

"Christianity is a religion for adult minds."[11]

"I am a priest, not a saint."[12]

---

7 Cyd Holsclaw and Geoff Holsclaw, *Does God Really Like Me?* (Downers Grove: IVP, 2018). The whole book is on this theme. The quote above comes from personal conversations in 2018.

8 Dale Moody, *The Word of Truth: A Summary of Christian Doctrine* (Grand Rapids, MI: Eerdmans, 1981), 110.

9 A.W. Tozer, *Knowledge of the Holy* (General Press, 2019), 11-12.

10 C. S. Lewis, *The Four Loves*, reissue ed. (San Francisco: HarperOne, 2017), 73-74.

11 Dorothy Sayers, *The Whimsical Christian*, quoted in Musing on Science, accessed June 29, 2022, https://musingsonscience.wordpress.com/tag/orothy-l-sayers/.

12 From the movie, *The Count of Monte Cristo*, based on the classic novel by Alexander Dumas, *The Count of Monte Cristo.*. This quote is spoken in the movie by Abbe Faria to Edmond Dantes.

Who are the Saints?

According to the New Testament, all believers in Jesus Christ are *saints*, a term that means "holy people" (Rom 1:7; 1 Pet 2:4-10). Every Christian is declared holy or set apart for God through the death and resurrection of Christ, and we now have the delight of surrendering to the sanctifying work of the Holy Spirit so that we live up to our holy calling (Rom 6; Eph 4:1-6). In other words, though there are appointed spiritual leaders and women and men of great character, there is no special category of "saint" or "super-saint" in the Bible; all Christians are called to a holiness rooted in love and gratitude.

But from the third century until today, *all* traditions of Christianity have created three tiers of sainthood and spirituality. At the top are the very religious: monks and missionaries. In the middle are the 'regular' pastors and priests. Finally come the other 97 percent, the "laity." Without denigrating godly authority and leadership gifts, this is not the picture of the beautiful community founded by Jesus and the Apostles. While God calls some to extraordinary places of service, all Christians are "full-time" for Jesus (Col 3:17-23).

As we considered all the dimensions of discipleship, we

were hesitant to label one as "spiritual formation" because *all* of life is under the leadership of the Holy Spirit. We have kept the title so we can focus on loving God as the foundation of all facets of life in Christ.

(Charlie): For several years now, I have asked all my seminary students and all audiences of leaders to stop using the terms "full-time ministry" or "full-time Christian service" because by default those terms elevate clergy while implicitly making other work "secular." As we shall see, there is no secular work in God's Kingdom; all good vocations and occupations are under the reign of King Jesus. By the way, it is good when pastors and missionaries receive full-time support! That said, 80-90 percent of all spiritual leaders around the world work more than one job—and are no less called by God.

Spiritual formation is the dimension most associated with discipleship—and rightly so. It is the critical starting point and energizes all other dimensions. We have identified eight outcomes indicative of the disciple's level of spiritual formation. Understand this: growth in Christ is possible for people of all backgrounds. The call of Jesus is not to sophistication but to true maturation; it is not to an elite status but to ethical stability. Not all people are intellectuals, but everyone can be biblically intelligent, growing in wisdom rooted in reverence for God (Prov 2-4). Let's explore the outcomes of growing closer to our loving Lord.

Remember, you can take the Assessment (www.discipleshipdynamics.com) at any time. The following summarizes the scoring for each dimension and outcome:

- 0-25: This is a new area for us or a real struggle.
- 26-50: We are growing but still have issues.
- 51-75: We are fairly stable and can keep improving.
- 76-100: We are mature and ready to help others.

O.K., let's learn about Spiritual Formation some more.

Outcome 1: Disciples Love the Word of God

Disciples are absorbed with the Bible (2 Tim 3:15-17) and have a good working knowledge of its contents. They can find answers to their questions in the Bible (Ps 19, 119). The Bible is a divine library penned by human authors over a 1,500-year period. It contains a Grand Narrative, a Big Story, in four chapters (Creation, Fall, Redemption, Consummation/Restoration—telling a story of design, disaster, deliverance, and destiny):

Chapter One is Creation: God's original *design* for humankind where worship and work are seamless and where dwelling with God and doing work with God are all part of a beautiful harmony (Gen 1-2).

Chapter Two is The Fall: Our sin has plunged all of creation and our lives into *disaster* from which we need rescue. The environment is marred, ethics are perverted, and both people and systems need liberation (Gen 3; Rom 5:12ff).

Chapter Three is Redemption: The Lord is on a mission of *deliverance*, reconciling, redeeming, and restoring, inviting us to join Him as we experience the grace of

Jesus Christ. All creation is being renewed and restored. This includes our assurance of eternal salvation and the promise of a renewed earth and heaven (Gen 12; Isa 61; 2 Cor 5:14-6:2).

Chapter Four is Consummation/Restoration: One day, it is our *destiny* that all will be well as we enjoy God's presence and fulfill His purpose completely in a redeemed community and creation (Rev 21-22).

All these chapters in the Big Story impact our lives, and as we grow in the Lord, we learn to read and interpret the Bible wisely.

One day a congregant came to me (Charlie) and asked about why the Bible had such difficult passages, like the suffering in Job, the despair of Ecclesiastes, and even Peter saying that Paul's words were challenging. I replied that we need the help of the Holy Spirit, history, and our community to properly read and apply the truths of God's Word. I also mentioned that there are different types of writing in the Bible call for careful thinking. Poetry is different from prophecy, and the Gospels and Epistles need context. This congregant felt grateful and said, "This sounds like work!" We laughed, and I said, "Let's get started!"

Yes, we need maturity, but the basic beliefs and behaviors of Scripture are *not* difficult to understand—even though they *are* difficult to obey sometimes!

Loving the Word of God does not mean we are superstitious about Scripture or that wisdom is only for a few privileged folks. It means that we read with a view to obedience and constantly learn the depths presented.

Part of loving God's Word includes learning the various disciplines that provide pathways for growth. Learned women and men have shared three basic disciplines with the church for two thousand years:

- *Reading the Word and aiming to read through the Bible over time.* This practice helps us see the panorama of God's grace and the unity and beauty of God's mission.

- *Studying the Bible in depth, alone and with others*, helps us mature as we discover how God's people have wrestled with similar issues and found help and hope from the Lord.

- *Meditating and memorizing allow God's Word* to get deep inside us and become a treasure chest from which we draw strength and wisdom. The applications the Lord gives us as we meditate are not new revelations or mystical interpretations but insights for character transformation.

Maturity in this outcome will keep us from distractions, help us focus on obedience, and empower us to encourage others.

Outcome 2: Pray Without Ceasing

Mature disciples have developed the capacity to communicate with God continually, regardless of the context in which they find themselves. They have developed the ability Paul speaks about in 1 Thessalonians 5:17 where he encourages the believers to "pray without ceasing."

"Why should I pray if God is in control and knows everything?" This question is asked often by believers, especially when facing difficult circumstances and delays in prayers being answered. Here is the biblical truth: our all-powerful, all-knowing Lord has decided to speak to us and through us, using our prayers as part of His will to bless the world! (Exod 32-34).

"Pray without ceasing" does not mean 24/7 talking or some kind of mystical state. This outcome directs us toward conversation with the Lord whenever we can. A personal prayer time every day is a great thing. In reality, busy new parents, running a business, and the other demands of life make the "sweet hour" of prayer difficult for many. We can also be honest with ourselves and begin limiting the amount of swiping on our phones, binge-watching TV, and other distractions. The goal is not a new legalism but enjoying God and participating in His mission.

Consider this again: the Almighty God, maker of heaven and earth, wants to speak with us and desires to hear us! We have taken this divine invitation to conversation and intimacy and turned it into a duty. Please notice Psalms 61-64: the songwriters complain, praise, testify, and ask deep questions. This is what prayer is all about!

As an illustration: Imagine, husbands and wives, that a friend offered you an all-expenses-paid week at the finest resort of your choosing in the world. All you must do is pack your bags and enjoy. Now, imagine one of the spouses saying, "No thanks. We see each other every day. No need for a special trip." The other spouse would be shocked, a bit hurt, and beg their partner to reconsider. "Darling, the chance to be alone and undistracted is wonderful. Let's accept the invite, please!"

Every moment, we are invited to enjoy God's presence and join Him on mission. Let's say, "Yes!" to this every day. Morning prayer is needed, and evening reflection will be transformative. Setting aside "quiet time" is valuable, but even if your schedule is crazy, you can find moments throughout the day to converse and intercede.

One day, a friend was working on his car and was underneath the engine on the ground. Suddenly, the car rolled over his legs. Miraculously, he escaped with no injuries but embarrassment. Later that day, he received a call from his mother across the ocean. She asked him if he was O.K., for at just the moment the car had rolled over his legs, his mother was praying for divine protection!

The Bible does not promise that we will never be afflicted, and prayer is not a set of magic words. But our Lord uses our personal cries and our community intercessions to change the world. Will we offer the cries of our hearts to the Lord, for others, and for ourselves?

We are invited to offer all our burdens, needs, and requests to God (Phil 4:4ff). We serve a loving Lord who gladly bears our burdens (Ps 62) and invites our intercession to make a difference in the world (Exod 32-34). Let's go past the duty and delight in the Lord.

Outcome 3: Worship in Spirit and Truth

Disciples are called to worship God under all circumstances. It is easy to worship when we are in the company of others who are singing God's praises, but it is quite another challenge worshipping the Lord when we are working at our jobs, or when we do not feel well (John 4:24; Rom 12:1-2; 1 Thess 5:16-22).

The words of Jesus and Paul in the Scriptures noted above forever change "religion as usual." To the woman at the well in John 4, Jesus offers a completely new way of understanding worship not only as an event or place but as an entire change of heart and a new orientation of life. Events in church buildings are good—and the Lord uses for changing lives, but worshiping God in spirit and truth encompasses all we do.

The Apostle Paul's words in Romans 12:1-2 and 1 Thessalonians 5:16ff also increase the scope of worship: all of life at all times and in all places is now an offering to God, in response to the grace of Jesus Christ. Worshipping in community—offering prayers and songs, learning and interacting as an act of gratitude for the Lord's goodness, remains vital. *The power of our worship together, however, is proportional to our personal decision to worship at all times!*

We were created for worship and work, to dwell with God and do His work in seamless delight (Gen 1-2; Rev 21-22). Our brokenness from the Fall created the sacred/secular, Monday/Sunday, worship/work divides.

We want to bring the following two challenges to God's

people with this outcome. *First, biblical and historical community worship is participatory, not passive.* Our prayers and singing, and our interactions and expressions of gifts, are the biblical normal. Too often the local church has exchanged engagement for entertainment. *Second, we need to offer our daily work as worship and consider all we do as important to God* (Col 3:17-23). Doing so will energize us, and, as we welcome the Holy Spirit's direct involvement, we will see the natural and supernatural come together.

Our friend, Dr. Roger Valci, wrote a little tract years ago called, "5 Minutes." He challenged his congregation to wait on the Lord for five unscripted minutes in each worship service. Over the next months and years, beautiful expressions of the spiritual gifts emerged, with women and men, young and old, offering Scriptures, songs, and insights that were in order and part of the orchestration of the Spirit.

Spiritual gifts are not only for our church meetings. The Lord is always with us, and if we are listening (see below), amazing expressions of His grace remain possible.

One of saddest sights in the body of Christ is when congregants engage in "worship wars," arguing over the music selections and atmospherics of corporate worship services. We are not going to engage those debates here! Our challenge is calling on all believers to praise God with their lips and their lives.

Will we offer our lives as worship each day, making every place we go a locale of holy love?

The great composer, Johan Sebastian Bach, always signed

his work and added three little initials, "SDG" – an abbreviation of the Latin phrase, *Soli Deo Gloria*—to God be the glory. May this be our constant song.

Outcome 4: Listen to the Voice of God

Jesus taught His disciples that His sheep are able to hear His voice and to follow him (John 10:27). This skill develops over time. As disciples grow in maturity, they can discern the voice of God and differentiate it from all the other voices that demand their attention (Ps 5:7-8; 32:8-9).

Right away, we must clarify an important point! Hearing God's voice is not the same as 'hearing voices!' The former is a delight; the latter needs psychiatric help. Yes, God can speak audibly; however, most often it is in the stillness of our spirits that we sense the Lord's comfort, conviction, discipline, and direction. A good way to understand this is to think of tuning an old-fashioned radio. In the old days, one used a dial to carefully adjust the radio to end the static and tune into the station. Over time, disciples learn to tune out the static and tune in to the leading of the Lord.

We must raise another issue: no more wonderful—*or* manipulative—statement exists than, "God told me." All believers can hear God's voice and gain wisdom, but sometimes people use inner impressions to control others or end conversations. Controlling leaders use this language to end debate. Sometimes, the insights of others can enhance our first experiences. Other times, we realize that we missed it as our own desires and emotions clouded our perceptions. Be encouraged! God is speaking. He has designed the Word, the input of others, and our continual seeking as pathways to precision.

One way we learn to hear the Lord speak to us is through pondering the Scriptures and by reflecting upon God's own nature and character. So many women and men have received direction as they pursued the Lord consistently.

I (Charlie) received my calling to mission and ministry in a normal time of reading and prayer. As I read Isaiah 60 and 61, I felt in awe of God's ways and works. Suddenly, I felt God's presence intensely and became aware that God was calling me to "arise and shine" and "bring good news" to the world.

First Kings 19 is a famous passage that contrasts God's "gentle whisper" with the huge sounds of nature (and the pagan gods associated with false worship). The Prophet Elijah was in great need of divine help. Even though he had just triumphed over false prophets, he was weary and feeling isolated; however, the Lord reminded him that there were other faithful followers of Yahweh. It was not thunder, rain, fire, or earthquakes, but the voice of God that humbled Elijah and led to his renewal.

A friend of ours offered all his business and investment efforts to the Lord and daily prayed for wisdom. He researched well, listened to advice, and the Lord blessed him and helped him support his family and many ministries. For a couple of weeks, he sensed change in some of his portfolio and saw signs for concern with certain stocks. One day in prayer, he sensed he was to sell a particular stock. He obeyed, gaining a small profit. Two days later, the stock plummeted downward due to bad management. My friend had no inside information, just careful thinking and prayer. God cares about all we do…will we listen?

May we become more aware of God's gracious promptings inside our hearts. Sometimes a yellow or red flag keeps us from hasty, misdirected steps or words. Other times, we have a sense of inner peace or a strong resolve to obey by faith, even if we do not see the picture clearly.

Outcome 5: Pursue Biblical Principles for Living

Another characteristic of discipleship is a passion to understand how the Bible applies to contemporary issues in the world today. Disciples display passion for biblical applications to life. Deuteronomy 6, Psalms 19 and 119, Proverbs 2-4, and many other passages tell us that disciples want to know the "ways of God"—the biblical principles for living in all dimensions of life.

Sometimes the Bible is direct concerning what the Lord prohibits and promotes. The Ten Commandments present a beautiful and comprehensive look at how God's people can live their lives as a thank you for God's grace (Exod 19-20). Adultery, theft, lying, murder…these are wrong. Honoring only the one true God, keeping the Sabbath, honoring parents…these are good. As we read further, the Lord gives guidelines for all dimensions of life and domains in society. This is why the poet of Psalm 119 writes 176 verses praising God for His commands, ordinances, statutes—all facets of the ways of God.

"Biblical principles" include direct commands and prohibitions, and reflective wisdom. For example, the Lord commands care for the poor and offers detailed instructions for gleaning crops, generous charity, and even a Jubilee to keep God's people from generational poverty. For Christians, though we do not live in the same culture and geography as ancient Israel, these details help us (along with New Testament teachings) to craft wise principles for living and effective policies for the common good.

The commands of the Law (Gen-Deut) are reaffirmed by the prophets and reflected upon by the sages of the Bible. The person and work of Jesus—His words and works and His saving work through the Cross and Resurrection—are the foundations for the apostolic teaching to the local churches.

God's ways help us from being captivated by the extremes of human philosophies and political ideologies. For the last two centuries, communal vs. individual emphases have battled for the conscience of humankind. The Bible says both are important. Personal diligence, private property, and moral responsibility remain essential for human flourishing. But this is not some kind of refined individualism, where our own fulfillment is the chief goal of life! The Bible also calls for care for the poor, stewardship of creation, sacrificial generosity, and concern for the welfare of the whole community.

Growing in God's ways also liberates us from legalism. Sometimes, with good intentions, Christians become more religious than Jesus. (See Jesus's strong words for arrogant religious leaders in Matt 23!) Love for God and neighbor will often lead to sacrifices as we are sensitive to the needs of others (Rom 14:1-17). At the same time, many believers feel frustrated with traditions that go beyond the demands of Scripture and that represent preferences, not principles (Gal 2-3; Col 2-3).

I (Charlie) remember when drums and guitars first appeared in morning worship in the summer of 1974. I was a new teenage Christian, and I saw people leave the church because of their distaste for the contemporary music introduced alongside the hymnal in worship. I was sad and could not understand why anyone would not enjoy the good music! Fast forward twenty-plus years, and I am in Nashville as part of a leadership conference. There was a young worship team leading songs with new rhythms and lyrics. They were biblical, and the community was worshiping, but I was not happy; I folded my arms over my chest and muttered, "You call this worship?" Suddenly, the Holy Spirit spoke to me as asked, "Aren't you behaving like the older people that left the church in 1974?" Tears rolled down my cheeks as I repented of my "tradition" and learned to "sing a new song" to the Lord.

"You will have many more crises of obedience than guidance."[13] Obedience to the clear will of God in Scripture remains foundational for sensitivity to God's voice and for His specific direction. Think about this: if we are walking in conscious disobedience, how can God trust us with the expanded influence and provision we desire? On the other

---

13 Campbell McAlpine, Sermon delivered at Calvary Community Church, San Jose CA, 1975.

hand, if we are doing well in applying God's truth, we can expect the blessings of wisdom (Jas 1:5; 3:17-18).

As we enjoy God's presence and walk in His purposes, our witness will shine, as we shall see in the next outcome.

Outcome 6: Share the Gospel Wisely with Others

Disciples desire to share the gospel with others in a way that draws people closer to the Christ rather than pushing them further away (1 Pet 3:15-16). Sharing wisely means we can convey the gospel story and our testimony with clarity and humility (Phil 2). The Five Dimensions offer a guide for good conversations.

When the words "evangelism" or "evangelize" arise, many people see street preachers, stadium meetings, or door-to-door activity. While these can be fine, sharing the gospel takes place mostly through conversations arising from natural situations at home, at the workplace, in the market, or other situations of everyday life. The great Church historian, Justo Gonzales, writes that the Christian faith transformed the Roman Empire one conversation at a time.[14] The work of missionaries really matters, and their work is sustained and expanded by believers sharing the good news and their personal testimonies.

Sometimes, we feel afraid to share the gospel because of past experiences:

- rejection from family and friends

---

[14] Justo Gonzales, *The Story of Christianity*, vol. 1, 2nd ed. (HarperOne, 2010), 63-65, 109-115.

- lack of confidence in our knowledge
- weird personalities being offensive
- getting labeled as being in a "cult"
- attacks from people hostile to Christianity

The good news is that we can humbly share about the Cross, the resurrection of Jesus, and our own walk with the Lord and trust the Holy Spirit to use our simple words as seeds for future conversions. We can also develop our arguments and intellectual abilities so we defend our faith wisely. This outcome is not about arguing but about affirming that we believe the gospel and desire that others meet Christ and find eternal life.

Please notice the word "wisely" in this outcome. We need God's leading so that we share in the right way at the right time. It is not a good idea to preach to fellow workers when you should be productive. Demonstrating compassion, good ethics, and efficient workplace habits may earn us the right to speak in private conversations with the permission of our colleagues.

With these qualifiers in mind, it remains vital that disciples actually do share their faith with others. For the last several decades, people have wrongly quoted St. Francis of Assisi with the phrase, "Preach the gospel at all times; if necessary, use words." St. Francis never said this, and he was a model of bold proclamation backed up with deeds of compassion in the thirteenth century. Friends, it is not enough to hope that someone may see our kindness or good works and spontaneously ask us why we are so wonderful. With the leading of the Holy Spirit, we actively look for divine moments when sharing Christ is the loving thing to do.

The first point in the list above is the real reason we often hesitate to share our faith. No one likes rejection. In today's climate of hostility and indifference to Christianity, people will accuse us of being intolerant simply for believing the truth and honoring the Bible. We must affirm liberty for all people while also holding out to others the gift of salvation in Jesus Christ.

A wise old teacher was sharing with students that patience, prayer, and responsiveness to colleagues and friends all pave the way for salvation. He told the story of sharing a different pointer to the truth of Christianity with a skeptic for two years. They debated kindly, and he slowly won the respect of his colleague. One day, he was asked for a new proof (about #99!). The teacher responded, "I do not have a new proof, but I believe God spoke to me today and brought comfort as a family member passed away." To his astonishment, the skeptical friend said, "I think this is the best proof so far." In a few days, this hardened critic gave his life to Christ!

By the way, coming to Christ *does* mean being part of the church. According to 1 Corinthians 12:13, believers are baptized into the Body of Christ and are concretely and relationally members with one another in the community of faith. Of course, we are not saying that joining a church saves us, but if we are followers of Jesus, we will enjoy fellowship in the local church—the next outcome we will explore.

Outcome 7: Enjoy Fellowship in the Local Church

Christian discipleship is a community experience wherein we allow our brothers and sisters in the faith to speak into our lives (Rom 12:1-8; 1 Cor 12; Phil. 2:1-4). Seeking out this fellowship with others is critical. This is more than weekly attendance in a worship meeting.

We live in a world where many say they "want community." In reality, they want connections convenient to their individualistic tastes. These same folks repeat cultural and political memes and phrases, claim they want justice, but when things get hard, they run away from the hard work of forging and sustaining relationships.

To be fair, some disciples have experienced wounding by church members and leaders and feel wary of any religious organizations. The good news is that Jesus is the healer, and He and will help us find hope and a willingness to re-engage. We do not advocate staying in abusive or destructive relationships or systems. We can affirm that Jesus desires all of us to experience the goodness of the community of the Holy Spirit—one united by faith, hope, and love.

My (Charlie) wife, Kathy, and I have served local churches together for over forty years. Kathy is a professional artist, the mother of three, and a creative and insightful partner in serving the church and community. Over the years, we have experienced serious emotional/spiritual abuse as part of church staffs. Certain senior leaders were emotionally unhealthy, theologically immature, and very controlling. With prayer, good counsel, and support from family and friends, we found new communities to serve and over time the Lord restored us inside. We know that disappointments are part of the risk of friendship, but the goodness of fellowship has more than compensated for the challenges.

The church global and local is a beautiful community with all classes and cultures welcome.[15] Whenever the Holy Spirit is poured out, there is a new sociology where people of diverse backgrounds find faith and friendship together.[16] Ephesians 2:11-21 declares that all human divisions are reconciled in the cross of Christ. Ephesians 3:10 reveals the Church as a prism of the light of the Lord, a source of beauty and wonder for all watching. The glory of God evidences when very different people become friends, and outsiders feel like insiders from the moment they walk into our homes and churches.

When we advise church leadership teams that desire health and growth, we ask three questions:

First, "Do you want to get well?" This echoes John 5 when Jesus asks the man paralyzed for thirty-eight years if he desires healing. Perhaps we feel so used to the unhealthy in our churches that we can hardly imagine what normal might be!

Second, "Do you want to grow up?" Based on Ephesians 4:1-16, this question opens the door to humility and

---

[15] Irwin Ince, *The Beautiful Community* (Downers Grove: IVP, 2021). This is the thrust of the entire work, and these thoughts were delivered in a Made to Flourish online conference in March, 2021.

[16] Amos Yong, *Who is the Holy Spirit? A Walk with the Apostles* (Paraclete Press, 2011), 95-145.

wisdom as we help leaders reimagine maturity and their important role in equipping the saints. It feels sad when so many in the church mature chronologically, but their character issues are stuck in adolescence!

Third, "Do you want to make a new friend?" A local church will only be as healthy as its members' willingness to welcome new sisters and brothers. Surprisingly, many Christians feel "saturated" in their relationships and consciously and unconsciously refuse to befriend new people.

In the 1963 film, *Charade*, with Cary Grant and Audrey Hepburn, Grant wants to ask Hepburn out and be part of her life. Hepburn's character, playing hard to get, responds, "I cannot have any new people in my life. Someone must die first." May the Lord expand our hearts for new friends and help us be hospitable and care for the many who are marginalized by society.

When I (Charlie) first walked into a gospel-centered church in 1973, I felt astonished at the warmth of people of all ages. My teenage friends had invited me, and people of all ages asked my name and expressed interest. Even though I was not a believer, I wanted to be part of this community! No one cared what clique I was in at school or what my grades or athletic abilities were—they cared about me. What a wonderful witness of God's grace and the work of the Holy Spirit.

Community involvement is complemented by the discipline and delight of solitude; are we comfortable being still and enjoying God and His creation? Let's explore this in the following dimension.

Outcome 8: Cultivate Solitude

In today's fast-paced world, sitting quietly and pondering the character and works of our God can prove challenging. We have come to associate worship with music and demonstrative praise, but learning stillness in the presence of God (Ps 46:10) remains vital for our spiritual wellness. Jesus practiced solitude when He withdrew from His disciples to be alone (Luke 6:12). Moses urged God's people to think deeply about the Law, and God told Joshua to ponder the Book of the Law continually as he led the people of Israel (Deut 6; Josh 1). Sitting alone to consider the magnificence of the God of the universe serves as a powerful discipline.

As we explore this outcome, we must assert that solitude does not equate with loneliness! Nor is solitude a discipline only for introverts. Solitude is not escape or isolation but a focused quieting of our inner being so we can find deep rest, biblical revelation, and personal renewal in the presence of the Lord. Solitude will come more easily to some than others, but it is a command for all to enjoy.

Solitude includes silencing all the noises competing for our attention. The folowing tips help in beginning this practice:

- Turn off and place all electronic devices out of hearing range and sight (unless you are on call as a first responder or facing family emergencies). This will be hard. Our minds and bodies have become wired to our devices, and we panic if our phones are not visible of if we miss a text. Please unplug.

- Sometimes music helps us to ponder the Lord and to worship Him, but we challenge you to gradually learn to be truly still without other stimuli. Enjoying and singing with great worship songs is another discipline altogether; it is part of worship, which we have already discussed.

- Begin with small steps—perhaps spend ten to fifteen minutes with nothing but an open Bible and a receptive spirit before the Lord. If you are a busy parent or running a business, this outcome will be practiced a few minutes at a time.

- As you pause, your mind will be filled with distractions, and the Adversary will try to invade this peace with distracting and distorting thoughts. Take authority in Jesus's Name, and bring every thought "captive" to the Lord (2 Cor 10:1-6).

- As you enjoy solitude, the Lord's voice becomes clearer, the Bible comes alive, and the ways of God are now delightful. Take the next several days or weeks to let Psalm 119 fill your heart and mind. Solitude will deepen your affection for the Holy Trinity, help you forgive others as you have been forgiven, and sense the Spirit's direction more clearly. (Notice all the other outcomes that are connected with this one).

(Charlie): A lifelong friend and pastoral colleague of mine, Doug Buron, was serving a church in the fast-paced Silicon Valley. He was inspired by the works of Richard Foster and Dallas Willard that encourage believers to cultivate a deep walk with the Lord through the classical spiritual disciplines, including prayer, Bible reading, and enjoying solitude. Pastor Doug's challenge was getting hard—charging business leaders to quiet their souls long enough to hear God speak to them.

One night, Pastor Doug asked all the folks in the weekly class to lay all electronics aside, pick up a regular Bible, paper and pen, and get alone with the Lord for fifteen minutes. In the previous week, Pastor Doug had taught his friends about hearing God's voice and about prayer. Now, outside of the group, he challenged them to have no external distractions, open the Word to Psalm 46, and ask God to speak. They all scattered to different quiet places throughout the church facility. About twenty minutes later, they reconvened. Almost every person was astonished—God really does speak when we listen! Many felt uncomfortable in the aloneness and silence, and it took them almost the entire time to still all distracting thoughts. Life change happened that night as solitude became a sanctuary to run to, not something to avoid.

We are Just Getting Started!

Many books on spiritual growth stop here. These outcomes are vital foundations for all that follows. Please, stay with us, and let's see how Jesus transforms every area of life. As we go to the next chapter, here is a focusing prayer that can help shape our deepening intimacy with our Lord:

"Gracious and loving Lord, thank you for being the

Almighty Creator and Abba Father. You are infinite and intimate; you care deeply about my life. Lord, I need your kind embrace and divine power. So many thoughts swirl in my head as anxieties try to rule my heart. I trust you, Father, and I rejoice that you are near. Lord Jesus Christ, thank you for being my King and for calling me friend. You are my Lord, the Bridegroom of your Bride, the Church. I welcome your Kingdom into every part of my life. Holy Spirit, thank you for your indwelling presence, bringing comfort and conviction each day. I need a fresh infusion of divine power as I seek to obey your commands and bring you glory as I serve others. Thank you, Father, Son, and Holy Spirit, for being so present and powerful. In Jesus's Name, Amen."

For Reflection

1. What are the blessings and challenges in your prayer life today?

2. How do you currently read and study the Bible for your own growth? What questions are in your mind?

3. How are you involved in your local church?

Life in 5D

Dimension Two:

Letting God Liberate Us from the Inside Out (Personal Wholeness)

"Spiritual and emotional health are inseparable."[17]

"The foundation of our inner healing and emotional health is a revelation of God's unconditional love."[18]

"We will all have reactions. Emotional maturity comes when we process our reactions and offer loving responses."[19]

Why Are So Many Religious People Unhealthy?

When anyone uses the word "discipleship," they automatically think of the spiritual disciplines that we covered in chapter 1. Disciples are "spiritual people," but they are also supposed to be psychologically healthy. I (Johan) spent

---

[17] Peter Scazzero, *The Emotionally Healthy Leader* (Grand Rapids, MI: Zondervan, 2015), 11-20. This quote comes from several of his works, and this chapter has an excellent summary.

[18] Dennis Woodsmall, A message given to the youth leaders of Calvary Community Church, San Jose, CA in 1977.

[19] Charlie Self, from my forthcoming book, *Thoughtful: The Pathway from Reaction to Response*.

years preparing for pastoral ministry, and after years of presiding over different local congregations, I came to realize that not all "spiritual" people are necessarily physically and emotionally healthy! I had many church members who loved the Lord on Sundays but who suffered from anxiety, depression, low self-concept, guilt, and the consequences of poor discipline in their personal and financial lives.

A wise college professor once suggested that to increase effectiveness when ministering to others, you must know God, know your Bible, and people. Like a three-legged stool, if you neglect one, you could fall on your face! The spiritual disciplines in the first chapter of this book help me to know God and know my Bible—a great start on the journey of discipleship. We must be familiar with the often unheard, secret voices, however, that drive people to unhealthy attitudes and self-defeating behaviors. This chapter is the second of our Five Dimensions and focuses on the voices that work against personal wholeness.

The second dimension of discipleship places attention on the realities in our own hearts, issues that reveal the level of emotional health. When the Bible says, "Love your neighbor as yourself" and "no one ever hated his own body, but he feeds and cares for it" (Matt 22:37-40; Eph 5:28-29), we see that reasonable self-care is part of being whole. We have identified eight discipleship outcomes that deal with the issue of personal wholeness from the Scriptures.

Outcome 9: Physical Health

Our bodies are referred to in Scripture as "the temple of

the Holy Spirit," and we are responsible to "glorify God in our body" (1 Cor 6:19). Through the New Covenant, our bodies have replaced the tabernacle in the wilderness of the Old Testament as the place where God resides. It therefore makes sense that Scripture admonishes us to take care of our bodies; the Lord lives in these "jars of clay!" (2 Cor 4:7-20) We can monitor several areas to promote this aspect of discipleship. This includes our Body Mass Index (BMI), our sleep habits, our exercise disciplines, our eating disciplines, etc. However, please do not let the Adversary shame you if you struggle with health, self-image, or weight. Help is near!

Physical health presents a tough area for many disciples because our culture sends so many contradictory messages. One minute we are told we can look like an Olympic athlete or supermodel if we eat this diet, follow that routine, or take certain pills. The next minute we are told that "fat-shaming" is wrong, and we should not judge anyone by their outward appearance (which the Bible does affirm).

The first voice that tends to mislead us is the voice that says, "My body has nothing to do with my discipleship! Discipleship is the stuff that happens on Sunday, not my fast-food choices or my lifestyle that is devoid of healthy physical activity." It is much easier to glorify God when the choir sings, and the "Spirit moves" on Sunday morning than when the advertisements on TV display succulent burgers, dripping with melted cheese and adorned with crispy bacon! We cannot think that the Holy Spirit's abode is uncomfortably flabby and unfit to house His glory! The fact that we must take responsibility to "glorify God in our body" (1 Cor 6:19) is an inconvenient truth!

Our bodies are complex. They reflect our genetic makeup, emotional histories, personal habits, and much more. Here is the essential principle: We should care for our bodies as God's temples, work with our doctor and wise friends cultivating healthy habits, and rejoice that we are loved by God regardless of our current health.

When I (Charlie) was twelve years old, my father wrote in the *Harvard University Alumni Journal* that I was "a fiery humanist and repressed basketball star (too short)." No amount of conditioning would help me dunk a basketball or compete at levels beyond high school. I had to accept my limitations, and I found new ways to exercise and enjoy other sports.

The world is not fair sometimes regarding health. Someone with terrible habits lives to age one hundred, and another person with amazing discipline dies at fifty from an undiagnosed heart condition. (Read Psalm 73 for an account of the unfairness of life; this is really helpful when we need to complain!) We cannot control all our circumstances, but we can care for ourselves as divine image bearers and those invited on mission with Jesus (2 Cor 5:11-6:2).

Sometimes the cause of maintaining one's good physical health is subverted by some of the "spiritual superstars" we read about in history: monks and nuns, spiritual leaders and missionaries who were constantly fasting, getting little sleep, and caring little about food or hygiene. Yes, God graciously used these women and men, but that does not mean we should follow their self-destructive examples. It is one thing to suffer community famine or poverty, and quite another to willfully deprive our bodies of the food, rest, and exercise needed to flourish.

Os Guinness wrote a small book in the 1990s entitled *Fit Bodies, Fat Minds*. He lamented the idolatry of the perfect body while neglecting intellectual growth. Oh, how we need balance here!

Here is the underlying motive for this outcome: we care for ourselves so we can serve God and others.

Jesus experienced all the same human limitations that we do: hunger and thirst, fatigue and frustrations, conflicts and crowds. Jesus developed as a regular human being, facing all the normal challenges of maturity (Heb 2-4). Though our Lord did not sin, he does understand our struggles and is therefore an empathetic High Priest we can run to, even when our bodies are not cooperating (Heb 4).

So, to all of us who share the burden of a Body Mass Index (BMI) over 25, and especially those of us that are over a BMI of 30, let us humbly confess that this is a constant battle. Our sleep habits, our exercise habits, and particularly our eating disciplines cry out for attention. *Discipline* is the core word of discipleship. Without slipping into a guilt trip, or increased anxiety because of an unfavorable BMI, let's humbly acknowledge that we are not there yet, but that we have tagged this issue with the label, "needs attention."

No one has a perfect body, so please feel liberated from trying to be anyone else. Let's become the best version of ourselves that we can.

Outcome 10: Positive Self-Image

Christian humility includes developing a healthy image of who you are in Christ (Rom 8:28-39; Eph 2:10; Col 3:1-4). Many cultural and social values—about the color of your skin or hair, how tall or good-looking you should be, or how smart or talented you are—conflict with biblical values and make people feel less important than others. Disciples understand that they are created in the image of God (Gen 1:26-28; 2 Cor 3:17-18). Disciples need to look into the mirror each day and rejoice in what they see.

The first questions people ask on this outcome is, "What about humility?" and "Isn't worrying about image a sin?" Well, appreciating that we are loved by God is not pride. Biblical self-denial is the yielding of our will to God's will and being willing to follow Christ regardless of the cost. *Self-denial is NOT self-destruction!*

The second voice that militates against our personal wholeness is the one we hear the loudest when we stand in front of our bathroom mirror and see the person everyone else in our world sees every day. What is the content of the message the person in the mirror conveys back to you? What do you say to yourself? That message can be unhealthy in two opposite ways.

On the one side there are those who, like Narcissus in

Greek mythology, fell in love with himself when he saw his reflection in the pool. His name became the core word for the psychological problem referred to as *narcissism*. Narcissists are people who have an excessive admiration of themselves and think that the whole world revolves around them. Paul warned that we must not think more highly of ourselves than what we ought, "but think so as to have sound judgment" (Rom 12:3, NASB).

However, "sound judgment" does not mean an attitude of disdain with what you see. Society places certain value judgments on attractiveness that tend to skew our thinking about ourselves—whether relative to the color or texture of our hair, the pigment of our skin, or the shape of our nose! People have common misconceptions about a perfect standard for the right height, correct body shape, perfect accent, or the best facial alignment.

Our early life shapes our view of ourselves, especially the vulnerable years from birth to five years old and then again as we mature into adults as teenagers. If we are loved, cared for, encouraged, and properly disciplined, we can have a hopeful and realistic sense of ourselves. Unfortunately, all of us have experienced degrees of rejection, heartache, disappointment, and mistakes from parents, family, friends, and others.

We must inject a vital insight here. If you have experienced serious emotional, physical, and/or sexual trauma, please seek professional help and ask for the prayers and support of trusted family, friends, and Christian leaders. If you are suffering from PTSD as a result of particular experiences (including military service), please find help. There is hope for living a healthy life as a follower of Jesus, and our Lord most often uses these wonderful resources as our pathways of healing.

Our journey toward a healthy self-image begins with knowing we are loved by God. No matter what we have been told by others, our Lord loves us so much that He went to the Cross and took on all our sins, sorrows, sicknesses, and sufferings—and even our unanswered questions, reconciling us to God by grace (Rom 5:1-11; 2 Cor 5:18-21). We were the joy set before Jesus as He voluntarily gave himself for us (Mark 10:45; Heb 12:1-3).

I (Charlie), like many young adults, struggled with self-esteem, especially in light of my family crises of parental divorce, and my mom's addiction and mental illness. I knew God loved me and that I had a decent brain, but I did not like what I saw in the mirror, and my emotions were all over the place. One day, one of my pastors took me to lunch and listened to my sorrows. He empathized deeply, then he did the unexpected, saying to me, "You are loved by the Lord. You are handsome and strong, made according to divine design. You are more than your brain, for God sees your heart. Rest in God's embrace, and you will find peace." I cannot say there have been no more struggles, but this was a watershed of liberation and hope! Thanks, Pastor Bill!

Peter King was a third-generation welfare child, and in third grade, his teacher told him he would amount to nothing. Sure enough, two of his businesses failed, and his loving wife and kids felt the tensions. At age twenty-eight, Peter wondered if his teacher had been right. Fortunately, he was invited to a Christian meeting by a friend. As he sat down, the speaker declared, "Remember, fellow-Christians, you are a child of the King!" Peter was a nominal believer, but when he heard those words, something happened inside. Generations of disappointment faded away. Personal failures were diminished, and hope was born. Over the next several decades, Peter became a successful business leader and advisor to governments. It all started with believing, "You are a child of the King."

Biblical self-esteem does not mean getting a participation trophy or being flattered. True self-worth comes from being made in God's image, knowing our worth in Christ, and living life as a thank you for God's grace.

Outcome 11: Gratitude

"Gratitude bestows reverence, allowing us to encounter everyday epiphanies, those transcendent moments of awe that change forever how we experience life and the world."[20]

When ten terminally ill lepers came to Jesus for help, Jesus displayed the graciousness of God's kingdom and healed them all. What a wonderful gift to restore these men to their families and their community! In response, though, when they got what they asked for, all but one disappeared

---

20 John Milton, quoted by Kelly S. Buckley, *Gratitude in Grief: Finding Daily Joy and a Life of Purpose Following the Death of My Son* (CreateSpace, 2017), 133

without even saying thank you (Luke 17). Scripture tells us that Jesus was perplexed and asked the one who came back, "Where are the other nine?" What a terrible disappointment that must have been for him!

Ingratitude is such an ugly characteristic. Did the nine who received healing somehow feel that it was their *right* to be healed? Did they simply take for granted it was their *good fortune* to be in the right place at the right time to have a saving encounter with Jesus? Did they think their healing was what was *owed* to them? Whatever their reasoning, they were responding selfishly. When we are ungrateful, we take for granted the good things we enjoy. It is based on a sense of pride and self-importance that somehow believes all of these things are owed because of one's position in life!

Disciples live as grateful people rejoicing in the profound blessings that they enjoy every day (1 Thess 5:18). We must acknowledge that when we are in the midst of pain and suffering, expressing gratitude is hard. That is why God gave us the Book of Psalms, though, so we can complain and pour out our hearts to God, *and* rejoice that God is present in all circumstances (Psalms 73 and 37). We can rest in God, assured that everything works together for our good (Rom 8:28).

Gratitude also arises from a sense of awe and wonder as we ponder the character and nature of our Lord and the magnificence of His creation. A friend of ours, Loretta Steiger, a wonderful Bible teacher, often encourages her students: "Never lose the wonder of who God is and all that he has given us."

A decade ago, my (Charlie) oldest son, Michael, joyfully participated in some medical outreaches in Ugandan villages: teaching hygiene, distributing medicine, and helping local nurses with technology and other resources. Michael was amazed at the gratitude of all the villagers for the simplest things. If the harvest was good, the roofs not leaking, and the water supply clean and steady, they were rich! As he and his team finished their week-long efforts, the children danced and sang, and the families prepared a feast for them. Their gratitude changed the lives of all who were there serving them!

Psalm 116 helps us frame our entire life as a thank you to God for His grace toward us. Let's pause and think about this for a moment. We survived birth and childhood—a huge percentage of humanity in history has not. We have seen God's protection and provision—we are healthy enough to read and reflect on this book! May we frame our good works, our obedience under pressure, and our endurance as gratitude to the Lord.

Life is hard. Real reactions to our struggles will include anger, fear, anxiety, and even despair. Learning to process (not ignore or repress!) our feelings and turn negative dispositions into positive aspirations remains vital for a flourishing life. Let's learn about this important part of following Jesus.

Gratitude is difficult in the midst of injustice and suffering. When the Bible tells us to give thanks in all circumstances, it does *not* mean being thankful *for* the circumstances, but grateful to God *in the midst* of the challenges. Here is an important theological insight: not everything that occurs in life is the direct will of God. Though God is sovereign over all, He has allowed great latitude for human freedom. Our Lord rejoices over our devotion (Zeph 3:17) and weeps over our disobedience (Jer 8:8-9:2). Jesus understands what it is like to ask, "Why?" and not get an answer as He took our sins, sorrows, sufferings, and unanswered questions on the Cross (Mark 15:33-34). What a wonderful Savior we serve!

Outcome 12: Manage Negative Emotions

Daily we experience such emotions as happiness, anger, frustration, fear, embarrassment, and amusement. These emotions typically trigger responses that are either healthy or unhealthy. Learning to manage our negative emotions is one of the tasks the Holy Spirit helps us with. He fosters affections of joy, peace, and patience when negative emotions flood in (Gal 5:22-23; Phil 4:4-13). Our first reactions are not sins; how we process our emotions will determine whether we will need to repent or rejoice. Maturity involves managing these feelings and turning frustration to faith, anger to positive action, and despair to determination.

Experiencing negative emotions is a normal part of life. Adam and Eve felt so distressed that they tried to hide from God after they failed Him miserably. Elijah, so depressed when Jezebel wanted to kill him, fled into the wilderness and wanted his life to end (1 Kgs 19). Even

Jesus experienced negative emotions. He asked three of His closest friends to support Him in His anguish, and they basically abandoned Him. *The Living Bible* quotes Jesus as saying, "My soul is crushed with horror and sadness to the point of death" (Matt 26:38). While He was praying alone in the Garden, and the full reality of His impending death sentence flooded over Him, He even began a passionate negotiation with His Father to consider the possibility of an alternative course of action.

Negative emotions can well up inside of us for several different reasons: feelings of guilt for some sin, a sense of abandonment, anticipation of danger or death, a fear of the future, and many more reasons. It is not possible to *avoid* negative emotions. Disciples do not ignore or deny that they experience negative emotions. Disciples learn to *manage* negative emotions.

Here is a strategy for managing negative emotions. *First, acknowledge that they are part of life and require a strategy to deal with them. Second, analyze how they got started in the first place: where did they come from?* If we don't get this piece right, we could end up providing a remedy that does not address the problem. It would be quite appropriate for someone who experiences negative emotions because of their sinful rebellion to confess their sin and to experience the peace of the Lord that comes from experiencing forgiveness. A person who feels abandoned would need to develop their faith in the loving provision of the Lord, and through that experience of provision learn about resting in the peace of the Lord. *Third, identify the cause, and find appropriate ways of managing how the emotions affect your behavior*. Whatever the cause, we can be sure that one of the tasks of the Holy Spirit in our lives is to foster affections of joy, peace, and patience when negative emotions flood in (Gal 5:22-23; Phil 4:4-13).

Our moments of depression may have many different causes. Sometimes depression has its root in lack of sleep or holding to an unbiblical or unhealthy cultural belief system. A young student who grows up in a very conservative, legalistic family and comes to the city to go to college can experience significant depression when she decides to cut her hair, go on a date, or wear jeans for the first time. A person who has been sexually violated or abused can also experience depression. A young man faces social rejection as he tries out online and in-person dating. We also have come to recognize that severe depression can have a biological or chemical cause. Clinical, consistent depression deserves professional help. At the same time, we have talked with many mental health professionals, and all of them say their caseloads would be greatly reduced if people had close friends and pastors in their life. Please do not isolate!

A dear friend and pastor we know was doing well in life and ministry and had no history of mental illness in the family. One day, he hit a wall and found himself in the emergency room. After several tests, doctors discovered a chemical imbalance in the brain and some problems with his endocrine system. With treatment, he was soon well; after a short time, he no longer needed medication. He continued learning, and over the years he helped many congregants and colleagues get the counseling and medical help they need. If your negativity persists, please seek help with your pastors and professional counselors. You do not have to be stuck emotionally. There is hope!

Christian hope is different from all other philosophies and religions. It is not fantasy or wishful (or wistful!) thinking. As we will see, God's hope transforms!

Outcome 13: Hope for the Future

The resurrection of Jesus is the source of our eternal hope, as we see in our Lord a preview of our future! We can feel confident in our eternal destiny and in the work of the Holy Spirit in our life today (1 Pet 1:3-4; 1 John 3:1-2). Learning to live by faith when we cannot see the future is a sign of maturity (Heb 11-12). One can easily forget that "all things work together for good for those that love God" (Rom 8:28-30) and begin to doubt that the future is secure in His hands.

The future remains a mystery. So many factors in our environment can impact our lives. Disciples are believers who have developed a level of confidence about a future filled with hope and faith. They have a sense that nothing the future may throw their way will prove impossible to manage. Hope is a 'trust thing.' Whereas the outcome in the previous chapter demanded skills to manage the impacts that the past could have on our lives, this outcome requires a level of skill to manage the unknowns of the future.

We (Charlie and Kathy) have faced several seasons of living

into the unknown. In 1984, with a new baby and seminary classes, our church faced financial crisis. I (Charlie) and four other pastors were laid off. A decade later, we left an unhealthy situation and spent several months waiting for new direction. As we write this book, another new season is dawning; the way forward is hopeful, but not clear. In all situations, the Lord proved himself faithful as we aimed to walk in faithfulness each day.

Christian hope differs from all other forms of hope, such as those found in other philosophies and religions. Such hope is not wishful thinking or wistful desire. Because of Jesus, we have an inner certainty of our eternal future; the presence of the Holy Spirit is God's "down payment" on the future—we start experiencing the future in the present (Eph 1:13-14). Deliverance, forgiveness, healing, and reconciliation are present realities as we allow God's presence and purpose to fill our hearts with hope. The Lord's healing presence also helps diminish the pain. We are not in denial; rather, we have a theology that embraces *both* glory and suffering. Sometimes we have amazing miracles, and sometimes we endure seasons of desolation (2 Cor 1, 5).

Fear of the future is a sign of distrust in Christ. Disciples displace fear with faith so it will not interfere with their maturing Christian attitudes and conduct. Disciples learn to manage anxieties and phobias with the joy of the Lord (Phil 4:4-13).

The prior outcomes relate to things in the past or future that invade our peace from the outside or from physical causes. This next outcome focuses on our responsibility for our decisions and the pathways designed by the Lord for inner peace—even when we err.

Outcome 14: Clean Conscience

Spirit-filled disciples must war against various spiritual attacks on their inner well-being (2 Cor 10:1-6). This discipleship outcome describes what to do when you face spiritual attacks from your past that attempt to rob you of peace. Spirit-filled disciples have learned to live with a clean conscience. No one alive can accuse them of wrongs that they have not tried to make right (Rom 12:9-19). Disciples have peace in their hearts about their past (1 John 3:21-23).

Another voice comes from our past to disturb our emotional well-being—guilt, the voice that constantly nags our conscience and grinds down our self-confidence. The Bible illustrates the impact of this emotional disturbance by using the metaphor of a court case (see Rev 12:9-11, ESV). Here is the scene: God is on the throne, and we are the defendants, being accused of violating the laws of God. The prosecuting attorney is accurately referred to as "that ancient serpent, who is called the devil and Satan" (v. 9). This scene portrays him as not playing by the rules, he is the "deceiver of the whole world" (v. 9). In the divine council, his case has no legal merit. His accusations of violations are all lies. The wrongdoings he accuses us of no longer exist; they were expunged. There was a full payment of the damages we are accused of being responsible for, and he acts as if he still has an air-tight case against those of us who are ignorant of the status of his case.

We should have known that there is something wrong in this court case. The Apostle John in his Gospel describes the prosecuting attorney quite accurately: "He was a murderer from the beginning, and does not stand in the truth, because there is no truth in him. When he lies, he speaks out of his own character, for he is a liar and the father of lies" (John 8:44, ESV). But here is the mystery of his deception: We believe him! We hear his evidence, we remember all those violations, we recall our culpability, and we stand in the dock and nod our heads in shame, "Yes, you're right…I'm guilty and worthy of your accusations! I agree I should be punished."

What a travesty of justice! Lies! It's all lies! We are *not* guilty. We make a grave mistake to side with the opposition to the divine council and concede our guilt.

The Apostle Paul sees this scenario as the context of a global spiritual warfare. He pleads with us to get out of that metaphorical courtroom because this is not where the warfare is taking place and says we must learn to fight on a different battlefield: "For though we walk in the flesh, we are not waging war according to the flesh. For the weapons of our warfare are not of the flesh but have divine power to destroy strongholds. We destroy arguments and every lofty opinion raised against the knowledge of God, and take every thought captive to obey Christ" (2 Cor 10:3-5, ESV).

The Christian doctrine of justification by grace through faith (Rom 3-5; Gal 2:16-21; Eph 2:8-10) is legal, moral, and personal exoneration as believers trust in the atoning work of Jesus Christ (Rom 3:21-31). The 'rap sheet' of humankind was placed on Jesus, and in His death is the erasure of our guilt and reconciliation (2 Cor 5:18-21). When we sin today, we do not lose our standing before God—we need to restore fellowship and allow the Holy Spirit to keep cleansing and transforming our lives.

As we trust God's grace for our past, we must also realize that keeping short accounts with God and others will increase our inner peace and strength. Ancient spiritual leaders would pause before bedtime and evaluate the day. If there were attitudes or actions that could have been better, they lifted those to God and determined to draw close and improve the next day.

Several believers we have helped over the years struggle with either legalism or license in their faith. Some with tender consciences go the altar to "get saved again" each week after falling short of God's commands. While confession and repentance are important, a true believer does not need to be "born again...again." On the other hand, some think that praying the sinner's prayer is a quick ticket to heaven and that they can sin with impunity. Such is *not* the attitude of a true believer (Rom 6). If we have died and risen with Christ by faith (Col 3:1-4), then our affections and action will be for God's glory and the good of others. We will stumble, but we can keep aiming to please God (1 Thess 1:1-5).

The ancient mothers and fathers of the Church practiced a discipline called *Examen*—the daily evaluation of attitudes and actions, desires, and thoughts. Welcoming the

Holy Spirit's examination (1 Cor 2), these believers sought the pleasure of the Lord. Of course, such scrutiny can also turn into unhealthy obsessions with unimportant matters, leading to a new legalism! Romans 14 and James 4 help us understand that we should walk in humble faith, not fear, and never violate our conscience, even if certain things are OK for others.

Christians often debate many "gray areas" around cultural practices. As stated already, believers must listen to the Lord and obey both the clear commands of Scripture and the personal direction of the Holy Spirit. For example, a believer who struggled in their pre-Christian life with pornography will be quite strict with what they permit for entertainment. Someone wresting with addiction must never take a drink, even if a friend is free to do so. A "strong" believer will adjust her or his behavior as it might lead to another falling away from their faith. This kind of sensitivity is not "holier-than-thou" legalism but liberated disciples enjoying God's grace and truth.

Outcome 15: Self-Discipline

Paul and Peter tell us that self-discipline is part of the fruit that the Holy Spirit actively cultivates in our lives (Gal 5:22-23; 2 Pet 1:6). Research provides us with insights into the benefits of delayed gratification. Being able to postpone immediate gratification in order to enjoy a greater reward later has been associated with a wide variety of mental and physical benefits.

Every person on planet earth knows we all have "a dark side." We do not need science fiction movies to tell us that. The Apostle John summarizes it well when he warns us against the "lust of the flesh, lust of the eyes, and the pride of life" (1 John 2:15). From an early age, we learn to fight for what is ours (using the word "mine" at a young age!); we seek to fulfill our passions through what we see, feel, and own. Disciples do not deny that we have temptations; we have lots of them! We do not deny the reality of seductive sexual attractions. We do not ignore the tantalizing delight of a hot chocolate sundae with real Belgian chocolates and home-made ice cream. Nor do we disregard the appeal of a brand-new sporty sedan with leather seats and all the electronic bells and whistles Silicon Valley can throw at us! We are not immune to these appeals to our base nature. The writer of Hebrews reminds us that Jesus understands all our temptations to turn to the dark side because He was tempted in every way, just like we are (Heb 4:15).

Spirit-filled disciples learn to *manage* temptations. Just like Jesus, we know we are going to be tempted, but also, just like Jesus, we know we do not have to give in to them. Delaying gratification of our wants, needs, and temptations is a skill we need to learn early. We teach our children to delay TV time till after they complete their homework. We teach teenagers about limiting their screen time. We teach young people who become aware of their developing sexuality to delay intercourse until after marriage. We teach students to suffer through the drudgery of studies and academic disciplines so they can reap the reward of graduating. We teach young married couples to delay spending more than they earn and to manage their debt.

(Charlie): One day a couple came to my office at the church where I served. The day before, they had surrendered their lives to Jesus during the morning service. We took time to rejoice in God's grace…then the tears started. They had lived together unmarried for eleven years and had four children. How could they come into alignment with the Bible? They knew they should have married earlier, and they wondered if God could help them.

I shared the good news: Jesus really does make everything new! They were from another city, so I referred them to a pastor and church and asked that they follow a new plan going forward. They agreed to remain accountable to a man and a woman in their new church, work with the pastor, and bring all their issues under Jesus's loving reign. They took ninety days to prepare for their wedding and told their children that their (temporarily) separate bedrooms were part of the special preparations for the celebration! They also received financial counseling and learned to live below their means.

One year later, they were married, debt-free, and able to purchase a home! All were enjoying their new church, and they called to say that the Lord gets all the glory.

We live in a world where everything is "supersized" and "Xtreme," and moderation is rare. Whether it is children eating vegetables before dessert, young adults saving money instead of using credit cards, or dating couples postponing sexual intimacy until the wedding day, self-discipline, though hard, is energized when the rewards are clear: better health, fiscal stability, a clear conscience—and divine delight.

One key to discipline involves making sure it is rooted in love, not just duty. When we know that our self-control pleases God and is for our good, it feels easier than if we do it only to stay out of trouble. This is especially true as we aim to manage our finances in ways that honor God.

Outcome 16: Manage Personal Resources

The way we manage our income, expenditures, and debt commitments is an excellent barometer of maturity (see Prov 11-12 for more wise financial ethics). When money becomes so important that it enslaves us to work too many hours a week, or when we live beyond our means, we are in a zone of spiritual danger (Matt 6:24-34). When Paul says we should not owe anyone anything except to love one another (Rom 13:8-10), he is giving sound spiritual advice!

When many read this, questions explode in their minds: "What about student loans?" "What about a mortgage for a house or a payment on a car?" In general, the amount of debt should be as little as possible and managed in a way that it can be repaid without undue stress. This said, many of us find ourselves in difficult financial straits. Sometimes, it is not our fault: loss of a job, medical bills, house repairs, and helping others can all add pressure. Even if we have made mistakes, the Lord is present to help. One more reality—raising kids and launching your adults into their futures is expensive!

John Wesley, the great evangelist and social reformer of the eighteenth century, said that believers should "earn all they can [ethically], save all they can [judiciously], and give all they can [generously]."[21] This great evangelist and social reformer was a wise business manager. In today's dollars, Wesley gave away at least five million dollars during his lifetime.

Here are some danger signs that you are not succeeding in this discipline:

- You often find yourself failing to pay your bills on time.
- You are denied credit at a store or a bank when you apply.
- You often find that you are short of cash.
- You are spending more than you should.
- Your credit score drops to unhealthy levels.
- You have to borrow money from friends or family to make ends meet.

Our local economy, age, skill sets, and opportunities all impact our earning power, but we serve a wise God who can help us find the way forward (Jas 1, 3). If we can

---

21 John Wesley, "The Use of Money," (The Sermons of John Wesley, Sermon 50), Wesley Center Online, accessed August 11, 2022, http://wesley.nnu.edu/john-wesley/the-sermons-of-john-wesley-1872-edition/sermon-50-the-use-of-money/.

decide ahead of time to tithe, save, live below our means, and look for ways to expand our incomes, we will see the blessings of the Lord.

There are many stories of the Lord redeeming personal finances as followers of Jesus apply biblical principles. The key is self-discipline, a clean conscience, and learning delayed gratification. Even with strict discipline, we can still face challenges, and we must not give our adversary any room for false guilt. God also enjoys celebrations, and faithfulness can include moments of feasting. Jesus's first miracle and the Cana Wedding (John 2) were symbols both of His messiahship as well as fun for the participants!

Here are a couple of encouraging insights as we bring our finances under the Lordship of Jesus Christ:

- Different callings and jobs will mean different income levels and stewardship responsibilities.
- God will provide all we need to fulfill His purpose in our lives.
- Our obedience prepares the way for surprising moments of goodness and grace.
- Sometimes we need to learn to receive as well as give, accepting help when needed and then giving help when we can.
- Every family must work out their particular economy with spouses sharing home and outside work responsibilities and forging agreement on the budget.

- Wealth can be created; we live in a world of abundance. There is not one pizza for eight billion people. We can bake more pizzas!

God created us to work with Him creatively as co-regents managing the world (Gen 1-2; Ps 8). Jesus is redeeming our fallen work, and in our daily labor we have a foretaste of future worship and work (Rev 21-22).

As we move from the disciple's inner life to enjoying healthy relationships, here is a focusing prayer you can pray to welcome the Lord into your emotional life:

"Holy and loving Lord, I need your healing today as I wrestle with so many feelings and thoughts. Please forgive my sins of anger and bitterness and my unholy rap sheet I keep against myself and others. Thank you that I am justified by your grace and welcomed into your presence through Jesus Christ. I forgive all who have wronged me, and I ask that you bless and forgive them. I repent of my tendency to bury my hurts and bad habits and ask for your love and power as I choose to walk in holiness that reveals I am a new creation in Christ. Thank you for your grace as I walk in my new identity and make wiser choices. In Jesus's Name, Amen."

For Reflection

1. What people or situations trigger serious emotional negativity? How are you seeking help for these challenges?

2. With the Lord's help, what are your hopes for the future? If this is a problem, who are you praying with to help shape your perspective?

3. Finances are always a sensitive issue. Are you tithing, saving, and budgeting? What can you and/or your family do to improve your situation?

Life in 5D

DIMENSION THREE:
Loving Our Neighbor Every Day (Healthy Relationships)

"I love mankind. It's people I can't stand."[22]

"We like the idea of *koinonia* [fellowship in the church], but the reality is harder."[23]

The third dimension of discipleship focuses our attention on our relationships with others, the practical expressions of "love your neighbor as yourself." We have identified eight discipleship outcomes from the Scriptures that deal with issues of healthy relationships. Both triumphs and tragedies in Christian life and mission rest on the quality of relationships.

---

22 Charles Schultz, "Peanuts" Comic Strip, November 12, 1959, Schmoop, accessed June 16, 2022, https://www.shmoop.com/quotes/i-love-mankind-its-people-i-cant-stand.html#:~:text=This%20line%20was%20spoken%20by,existence%2C%20and%20the%20good%20life. (Schultz has his character, Linus Van Pelt, make this statement.)

23 Rick Howard, Lecture delivered at Calvary Community Church, Fall, 1976.

As a reminder, you are welcome to take the assessment at any time for a current snapshot of how you are doing in all areas of life as you follow Christ (www.discipleshipdynamics.com).

Outcome 17: Love Intimately and Unselfishly

People who have experienced hurts in their relationships tend to resist close relationships with others. It becomes difficult for them to allow people to come close to them because in their experience, people who come close tend to cause pain and bring disappointment. The typical response for such people is to keep others at a distance, but this is not healthy. In the kingdom of God, we need the fellowship and support of the family of God. Learning to love intimately, even when we have been wounded, is a sign of emotional health and maturity (1 Cor 13; Phil 2:1-4).

The Bible speaks of three kinds of love—all gifts of God. The first is friendship, or "brotherly/ sisterly love" (*phileo*). This is the mutual affection and respect of people not gazing at each other but looking at life in the same direction and helping one another. This love is one of the normal expectations for believers in the local church (2 Pet 1).

The second type of love is attraction (*eros*): the love focused on desire for another. This is most often understood as sexual attraction; in the boundaries of covenant marriage, it is a good gift from God (Song of Solomon). In our world today, *eros* is often the first love and if mismanaged has the potential to distort all others.

The third love is *agape*, the love that unselfishly desires and wills the best for others. This is the love of 1 Corinthians 13: kind and patient, enduring and sacrificial, wanting the best and persevering through difficulties, and keeping no "rap sheet" against others. This is the love that sent Jesus into the world to die for our sins (John 3:16-17; 1 John 3-5). This love is only possible for believers if they know they are loved by God (see Self-Image outcome above).

Christian love extends to all types of relationships, with believers wisely desiring and doing what is best for others. In marriage, spouses aim for their partner's flourishing and discover their joy is greater than it would be if they only think of their own needs. Friendships are strengthened as brothers and sisters challenge and encourage one another. Colleagues at work—whether believers or not—will appreciate our efforts (see the Teamwork outcome in the fourth dimension, Vocational Clarity) as we unselfishly aim for excellent service.

So many problems in life arise for disordered loves, especially when *eros* displaces *agape*, and we see people as objects of unholy affections—whether anger, lust, envy, or condescension. When we realize that each person exists as a divine image-bearer for whom Christ died, we can begin disciplining our thoughts, feelings, and actions according to God's love instead of according to momentary passions.

Christian love is under assault in many circles, especially among advocates of alternative relationships that affirm sexual intimacy outside of marriage. So much of social media, literature, film, and music is glorifying what the

Bible says is destructive for humankind (Rom 1:18-32).

How do we begin ordering our loves well? As mentioned, we must first receive God's love revealed in Christ as the source of our self-image and security. With this foundation, we are liberated to love well as we decide ahead of time that

- everyone that we meet as a divine image-bearer (Gen 1:26-28) and worth the sacrifice of Christ (Heb 12:1-3)
- each person as a brother or sister, thus keeping sexual attraction in check; and
- the goodness of our desire for the opposite sex and keep fulfillment within the bounds of biblical marriage.

Let's take a moment to consider our sex-charged world of advertising, social media, and loud voices saying, "Anything goes!" One professional I (Charlie) spoke with in 2008 said to me, "I have a right to sex, without consequences." Wow! He acknowledged that sexual intimacy must be consensual, but he was gravely mistaken that there are no consequences. In 1 Corinthians 6 and 2 Corinthians 6, Paul reminds believers that their bodies are temples of the Holy Spirit, and that sexual intimacy includes a union of spirits (our inner being), not just bodies. If disciples decide to love their neighbors, they will preserve sexual intimacy for marriage, and when attracted to someone (it will happen often!), regard her or him as a sister or brother. This is freedom!

Outcome 18: Forgiveness

Jesus calls His disciples to forgive others, as God has forgiven them (Matt 6:7-15; Luke 7:41-50). Forgiveness has received great interest from researchers in the past few years. It is now widely understood as a healthy personal response to hurt, as well as a fundamentally important spiritual-theological concept. The capacity to forgive requires that someone have inner strength and a willingness to be humble in a relationship scarred in the past by painful interactions.

Forgiveness does *not* mean excusing the perpetrator or erasing the memory; it is a divinely-aided choice to treat the person as we would want to be treated by God. It is a precondition of our own prayers being heard, and it remains essential to the community of faith (Eph 4:22-31; Col 3:1-16). Forgiveness does not mean that we place ourselves in dangerous or unhealthy situations of abuse. When we forgive, we place the guilty party in the hands of a just and loving God, and we can go forward in life, experiencing healing and hope.

In the late 1980s, I (Charlie) was teaching evening classes in a Bible college with many older pastors and lay leaders as students. In a typical class of fifteen, we would have five to seven different cultures, and the experience was enriching for all. One night, Pastor John, pastor of a Cambodian church about ninety minutes away, shared his story. Pastor John was a survivor of the Killing Fields of Cambodia in the 1970s, when the Communist Khmer Rouge killed almost two million people. He watched his family be killed, and he barely escaped with a few others. Fast forward to the present: Pastor John was praying with people at the altar of his church one Sunday. He noticed a repentant man weeping before the Lord, begging for forgiveness. As Pastor John went to pray for the man, their eyes met, with immediate recognition: here was one of the Khmer Rouge soldiers who had killed many in his village! The man asked if he could be baptized. A few weeks later, redemption and forgiveness were celebrated in a refugee church as this former guard declared Jesus as Lord of his life!

Let's pause and examine our hearts—right now! Do we have a rap sheet toward those who have hurt us? Are we deceiving ourselves as we pretend to forgive while still wrestling with bitterness? Remember, we are not excusing what others have done (or our own sins, for that matter). We are choosing to let go of anger and desire the best for the one who hurt us. Healing from serious trauma takes time, and good boundaries and protection remain important. For most believers, communion serves as an ideal time to make things right with others (1 Cor 11), so we can enjoy the grace of the bread and cup with a clean conscience.

Prayers of blessing help us overcome bitterness and resentment. As we ask God to bless those who do not deserve it (after all, they hurt us!), our hearts change, and the Holy Spirit uses our intercession for the good of the person in need of grace.

Outcome 19: Marital Intimacy and Unity

The marital bond is the closest human relationship any of us could enter into (Gen 2:23-25; Matt 19:1-6; Eph 5:18-33). The development of intimacy and unity in marriage requires a maturing set of skills that include outcomes from all dimensions in this assessment. One could say that the level of marital intimacy is a good barometer of progress in all the other dimensions.

Three critical principles exist for cultivating intimacy and unity in our marriages. First, *the married couple must consistently pray together as husband and wife*, apart from grace over meals, bedtimes with kids, or in crises. The experience of God's presence together (no prayers disguised as lectures, please!) will build a foundation for conversations, decision making, and conflict resolution.

The second key has two parts: (1) *Each spouse must believe in and support her or his partner's calling*; and (2) *God has a shared mission for married couples (and their families if they have children)*. For example, Jamé is excited to support his wife, Jennifer, in her consultation work and counseling ministry. Jennifer is delighted to encourage Jamé's pastoral, consultation, and writing efforts. But there is more! Jamé and Jennifer have a shared mission that uses all their gifts and brings something new to the world. They are both dedicated to wholeness in persons, organizations, and communities, and they bring a vision together that helps change the lives of many.

When I (Charlie) was a staff pastor of a large church, a couple came to the altar and asked that I pray for their marriage. I was happy to bless them and ask for the Lord to meet them. They both wanted a good marriage but did not know how to overcome childhood patterns and the rejections of young adulthood. After we prayed, I recommended a great counselor, and they agreed to start down that positive pathway. I also asked them to pray together for five minutes each day—no lecture-prayers, no special language, just praise to God and blessings toward each other. The next week they came to the altar beaming. "We prayed three times this week!" I asked how they felt, and the wife said, "Things that were such a big deal and led to fights...I am seeing them differently now." The husband responded, "I am asking her how I can help and show love better. I thought she wanted flowers...and those are OK, but what she really wants is having the trash taken out and undistracted time in conversations." The next week, they shared that they had prayed almost each night and were ready for counseling. They were holding hands and happy together.

Our adversary the devil attacks marriages continually. Little spats turn into name-calling and wounded hearts. Social media implants thoughts that we can "do better" with someone else. Unhealed memories and traumas from childhood invade our hearts. Emotional and economic pressures bring great stress. Raising children and launching young adults are challenging on a good day!

The outcome of forgiveness is vital here, so that disputes do not become resentments and part of the emotional "rap sheets" we mentioned earlier.

As we listen to Jesus, learn about each other, begin articulating shared values, and keep no record of wrongs, we can build healthy marriages.

Outcome 20: Manage Sexuality

Managing one's sexuality presents an obvious interpersonal challenge that every person faces. The ancient Israelites faced pagan idolatry that expressed itself in sexual immorality (Hos 10-12). New Testament believers needed to learn stewardship of their bodies as they came to faith (1 Cor 6; 2 Cor 6). From adolescence to the point where we finally settle with our life partner, we typically face many struggles. The biblical standards are clear, but hard: celibacy for singles and fidelity in covenantal marriage of one man and one woman.

We live in a world of gender, identity, and sexual confusion, even inversion. "Anything goes" seems to be the song. Upholding the standards of the Bible and lifting up the hurting are both needed.

In first-century Corinth, one could not walk down the main street without being confronted by sexual temptation at every turn. Temples to Aphrodite had hundreds of prostitutes waiting for "worshipers" to come in. New Christians had to learn that the spiritual and physical components of their lives are united, and one cannot live a life of enthusiasm in church and bad ethics at home (1 Cor 5-6; 2 Cor 6).

When I (Charlie) was a new believer, I wanted to honor God with my thoughts and actions but struggled with impure thoughts at times (pretty normal for teenagers!). What helped me not be a slave to sinful patterns of thinking was realizing that every woman I saw was a sister, someone's precious daughter, and someone's present or future spouse. Friendships became delightful, and fellowship and working together free from tension served as my new normal. Freedom here is more than saying, "No!" to bad thinking or Internet surfing; we must say, "Yes!" to the image of God in others and desire their best.

Biological sex is a given. We are human beings made in God's image and given a job to do as a biological male or female (Gen 1:26-28; 5:1-2). In our fallen world, expectations regarding the gender roles of women and men vary widely with culture and economics; however, at no time and in no cultures has there ever been confusion about one's sex! Apart from rare birth anomalies, all persons are born with genetic and physiological evidence of their sex.

"Gender identity and fluidity" is a postmodern phenomenon and sows much confusion among emotionally vulnerable people. What was a psychological pathology years ago called "body dysphoria" and led to serious struggles, is now a celebrated, confusing array of terms that are continually changing. There is concerted effort by some to reinvent the human person and increase state control over family life.

How can we be morally strong and yet sensitive to the people around us? We must affirm biblical truth and acknowledge that while God's standards of identity and ethical behavior are clear, personal experiences are complicated. As we become secure in our new identity in Christ, we will be able to encourage others on the same journey. God's people must treat every person with dignity and love.

Our friend, Kent Paris, of Nehemiah Ministries has been helping women and men with their identities and traumas for nearly four decades. Gender confusion, same sex attraction, and other unhealthy affections are often rooted in emotional and physical abuse, or in the deceptions of a godless society that invade at vulnerable moments. Adolescence is hard on a good day. Imagine if a young woman or man is not very popular, struggles with their body image, and experiences bullying. It is not a great leap into the embrace of radicalized communities that welcome "exploration." Only Jesus offers full healing, hope, and identity that are stronger than the temptations rooted in hurt or rebellion.

We hear many voices agitating for justice and calling on the privileged to care for the historically marginalized. The Bible calls for compassion, and all who follow Jesus have the delight and honor of caring for those who history and society deem "outsiders."

Outcome 21: Sensitive to the Marginalized

Another outcome one does not see often in the discipleship literature is the example of Jesus relating to those rejected by society (Matt 25; Luke 7). It feels easier to associate with those who fit into our concept of "normality," but Jesus typically associated with the abnormal, the poor, the outcasts, and those who lived on the fringes (Luke 19). The marginalized include these groups and can extend to any group considered on the "outside" by society.

Compassion entails more than pity. Believers offer dignity, love, and respect to those who feel left behind, for they are divine image-bearers and worth the redemptive love of Jesus Christ. Helping people out of poverty and deep pain and into flourishing involves more than money or programs; it requires relationships of mutual love and respect. Every story we hear of someone "overcoming the odds" involves faith, some self-discipline, *and* the help of others.

"Being s ensitive to the marginalized" is not paternalism or a few checks written at fundraisers. Care involves intentional friendships across class and cultural chasms. In addition to personal connections, care involves working to improve systems so that all have access and opportunity to flourish. If you are a leader in the local church, it also means deliberate steps that foster hospitality to all; it *also* means intentional work so that all facets of church life are informed by the diverse experiences and perspectives of all groups.

Robert Woodson Jr. has helped local communities flourish for decades. Over three thousand groups and localities have benefitted from his catalytic work. In his book, *Lessons from the Least of These*, Woodson articulates the importance of place, real relationships, an entrepreneurial and ethical spirit, and much more for lasting change.[24]

---

24 Robert Woodson Jr., *Lessons from the Least of These* (Bombadier Books: 2020).

Brian Fikkert and his team at the Chalmers Center have been empowering individuals and communities toward flourishing by attending to the whole person and moving from charity to development that is sustainable. Fikkert's books, *When Helping Hurts* (co-authored with Steve Corbett), and *Becoming Whole* (co-authored with Kelly M. Kapic) offer detailed insights on the spiritual, empirical, and relational facets of transforming compassion.[25]

Amy Sherman's books, *Kingdom Calling: Vocational Stewardship for the Common Good* and her new release, *Agents of Flourishing: Pursuing Shalom in Every Corner of Society*, challenge us toward intentional relationships and systemic efforts that change power dynamics and opportunities and unleash the potential of every person.[26]

John Wesley told his Methodist members in the eighteenth century that charity must include friendship. Will we listen and learn, then love and serve those very different from ourselves? Such is normal Christian living.

Caring for the marginalized must not turn into condescension toward those on the outside. Jesus died and rose again for a Church that is a beautiful community of poor and rich, all colors and cultures, and every religious background. Every new sister or brother added to a local church is a living stone (not a uniform brick) added to a beautiful house God is building1 Peter 2:5. James 2

---

[25] See Brian Fikkert and Steve Corbett, *When Helping Hurts* (Chicago: Moody Press, 2014); see also Brian Fikkert and Kelly M. Kapic, *Becoming Whole* (Chicago: Moody Press, 2019).

[26] See Amy Sherman, *Kingdom Calling: Vocational Stewardship for the Common Good* (Downers Grove: IVP, 2011). See also Amy Sherman, *Agents of Flourishing: Pursuing Shalom in Every Corner of Society* (Downers Grove: IVP, 2022).

challenges local churches and every believer to not show favoritism toward the wealthy or the "insider." Instead, all are welcome, not only to a pew on Sunday, but into our lives every day of the week.

Outcome 22: Hospitable

One of the signs of spiritual maturity (and a qualification for spiritual leadership in the church) is the ability to extend hospitality to others, especially those who would not be able to reciprocate the kindness (1 Tim 3). In a world where it is much easier to live in your own private cocoon so no one will disturb you, the Christian virtue of hospitality offers an alternative. The New Testament Church was known for their hospitality and new friendships around mealtimes (Acts 2:42-47). Using your home to welcome others is a valuable ministry.

Perhaps you do not have a home or do not feel qualified to entertain. Relax! Hospitality means opening one's heart and spending time with others without desiring anything in return. This can be done a variety of ways. Are we creating places and spaces for people to feel at home with us and grow in the Lord?

Our (Johan and Charlie) friends, Brett and Lyn Johnson, have been equipping marketplace missionaries around the world for decades. In their homes in South Africa and the US, they have hosted hundreds of people for an evening or for months. Lyn equips women and men for hospitality through her "Heartistry" courses and by example. One of their main principles involves uniting simplicity with quality. Hospitality serves as an expression of God's love and a display of the Table of the Lord. One may have simple ingredients and furnishings, but attentiveness to guests and offering our best reflects our Lord who gave all for us and invites us, "Come and dine."

Let's expand our vision of hospitality to our local churches and workplaces. Are guests welcomed and known by name as they come to our church gatherings? Are newer or quieter employees invited to share their wisdom and help craft the future? If we are managers or leaders at work, are we setting tables that engender conversation and collegiality, or are we too busy and just zipping through the day? Even online meetings can be friendly and warm. In our churches, how long does it take for new congregants to feel a part of the family?

(Charlie): Kathy and I have enjoyed many church and family tables around the world. There is nothing quite like a potluck in a home or fellowship hall. When we were missionaries in Belgium in the early 1980s, we were hosted by East Indian, Swiss, Italian, Chinese, and Belgian students (the school had students from twenty-seven nations). What a foretaste of heaven!

All these relational outcomes are rooted in holy love. As the Lord transforms us from the inside out, we can extend friendship and find our affections and actions aligning with the Bible and empowered by the Holy Spirit.

Most discipleship books and guides stop here. But wait! There is more! Our discipleship extends to our personal purpose and daily work because our Lord cares about all we do.

Pray this focusing prayer for our relationships:

"Holy Lord, thank you for the many relationships in my life. Please help me manage them well. Keep my mind and heart pure and help me look for ways to serve those in my immediate circles of influence. I offer you my history of hurts and ask that by your Holy Spirit you will speed healing and liberation to my soul. Search my heart, O God, and reveal any hidden bitterness or resentments I need to bring to the Cross. I bless my family members, work colleagues, neighbors, and acquaintances. May your love and joy radiate through me as I learn their stories and look to bless them. In Jesus's Name, Amen."

For Reflection

1. Do you have family and friends who will help you process relational hurts and encourage new friendships?

2. Are you nourishing current relationships and remaining open to a new friendship?

3. How is the Spirit speaking to you about compassion for and friendship with people very different from you?

DIMENSION FOUR:

Walking in the Good Works God Has Designed for Us (Vocational Clarity)

"Today's discipline shapes tomorrow's destiny."[27]

"We need to unleash the vocational power of every member of the congregation for the common good."[28]

"While we honor religious callings, God's kingdom advances through the apostolate of the laity, with each person important to God and the world."[29]

The fourth dimension of discipleship reminds us that the Holy Spirit is poured out on all believers, and not only clergy are called of God (Acts 2:4ff; Eph 4:1-16). The word *vocation* means "calling." Every person who is a follower of Jesus Christ has been entrusted with a unique set of

---

27 Charlie Self, first used in a talk to doctoral students at the Assemblies of God Theological Seminary, 2019.

28 Amy Sherman, from a talk given in 2012 at the Acton Institute.

29 Pope John Paul II, "Jubilee of the Apostolate of the Laity,", November 26, 2000, Vatican, accessed August 11, 2022, https://www.vatican.va/content/john-paul-ii/en/homilies/2000/documents/hf_jp-ii_hom_20001126_jubillaity.html

gifts and talents that they must invest in service to God and others (Rom 12:1-8; Eph 2:10). These callings include our daily work but often are broader and deeper than how we earn our daily bread. Please read the special supplemental essay, "Vocations and Occupations," at the end of this book. We group eight outcomes under the Vocational Clarity dimension.

Outcome 23: Know the Dignity of Our Labor

Work is not the result of the curse in Eden (Gen 3). God invited Adam and Eve to work with Him to create value, produce crops, and manage the earth—*before* they sinned (Gen 1-2). Eden was full of grains, fruits, and metals for creative humans to develop and enjoy. God cares about our work because it gives us a purpose in life and contributes to God's glory, the good of others, and the expansion of His Kingdom (Matt 25).

"But what about the drudgery and boredom I feel in my work? It is so repetitive, and I need two showers at the end of my shift. How is there dignity in that?"

Friends, in a fallen world, we are not going to love every job or every part of a particular job. *Here is a definition of work: it is all meaningful and moral activity apart from leisure and rest.* The janitor in the airport makes our trips much more pleasant. Cleaning out cement trucks will prepare the way for someone's home or business to have good concrete in the future.

Dr. Kent Duncan, a pastor in rural Kansas, taught a congregation of blue-collar workers the importance of their work as worship before the Lord and as part of God's work in the world. He received this testimony from one congregant:

"My job is attaching labels to cans of dog food. Until Pastor's sermon series, all I knew was that this job was the way I fed my family and gave my tithe. The real spiritual work was my Sunday School class. After hearing Pastor, I started praying for my co-workers and blessing them. I also realized that every can of dog food represents a family with a pet and I was part of their happiness. My new attitude was noticed by my bosses and now I am a supervisor. I am happy they are listening to my ideas on improving our processes and employee morale."[30]

As I (Charlie) travel and serve leaders, churches, schools, and organizations, I ponder the number of people that help me get from one location to another. It is an extraordinary economic choreography! Let's review this:

- the rideshare driver (who is served by gas station attendants, care sales personnel, mechanics, etc.);
- the baggage handler who meets me outside the airport doors;
- the counter personnel as I check in;
- the janitor who keeps the restroom clean;

---

30 Kent Duncan, "The Holy Spirit Goes to Work: Facilitating Marketplace Ministry in a Blue-Collar Context" (D.Min. project., Assemblies of God Theological Seminary, Springfield, MO, 2015). This quote is from Dr. Duncan's public presentation of his findings, delivered at the Assemblies of God Theological Seminary in 2014.

- the baristas and waiters who give me coffee and food and the connected workers delivering the goods, preparing the food and cleaning the spaces;
- the gate personnel;
- pilots, flight attendants;
- mechanics—Thank you that we fly safely!
- baggage handlers and the folks directing the plane;
- the person getting the gate to the plane; and
- then repeat these processes at the second location!

Now take this modest example of twenty-five to thirty people directly involved and add the indirect computer programmers, shareholders, executives, construction workers who built the airport, etc.

Friends, there is no unimportant work. Before God, what matters is the value we create, not just the money we generate or make. Parenting (and grandparenting, foster parenting, being a nanny, etc.) is work. Volunteering is work. Work can be paid or unpaid. Work includes positions of labor and leadership that takes place at home, in offices, in factories and fields, online, and in person.

Mark Green of the London Institute of Contemporary Christianity, at the Capetown commitment Conference in 2010, sponsored by the Lausanne Committee for World Evangelization, shared that our daily work is the "frontline" of our being on mission with Jesus for the reconciliation and restoration of our world.

Outcome 24: Sense of Calling

Allied to the importance of work is a real sense of calling, an understanding that whatever I do, I am engaged in Kingdom work (Col 3:17-24). It is an acknowledgment that God has called me for a particular purpose (Eph 2:8-10).

As mentioned, under our Resources section, Charlie has an important article on "Vocations and Occupations" that helps to distinguish and integrate our calling and our daily work. We are always more than our job description, yet our daily work is where our character is refined and our calling expressed.

In the New Testament, there is a little letter at the end of the Apostle Paul's writings called Philemon. It is the story of Paul asking his friend to receive his runaway slave, Onesimus, back into his heart and home—not as a slave but as a brother. This work is considered one of the foundations of the abolitionist movement and a vital apologetic for equality among all classes and cultures. But wait…there is more! Year later, some theologians believe that Onesimus is the bishop over the region where Philemon lived! Onesimus has a calling to leadership even if for a season his day job was household slave.

A biblical sense of calling does not mean we should passively hang out and expect the world to bend to our dreams. This sense of calling is a gift from God and is discerned and refined as we listen to the Lord, stay in Scripture, participate in church, go about today's work, and explore our gifts and talents. (Notice all the connected outcomes here!)

Today's young adults face real challenges as they finish school and go into the job market. Despite many available jobs, some grads feel angry that their degree did not bring instant prosperity. Here is the good news: for followers of Jesus, God will always have a pathway of sustainability; however, it may involve seasons of labor in unexpected places while allowing the Holy Spirit to refine character, clarify calling, and add disciplines and skills needed for success.

A local church pastor who also works as a restaurant manager is not less a pastor than someone paid full-time by their church. That pastor's vocation is *pastor*, and their occupation is manager. Pastoral gifts can be expressed outside the church gatherings!

One large church tried an experiment for one year. All four full-time pastors took full-time jobs outside the church, rotated church duties, and delegated more authority and responsibility to lay leadership. They rejected the notion of "secular" work and offered all their activities to God as worship (Col 3:17-23). At the end of the year, the church had grown by 20 percent, offerings were higher, and many more new believers were baptized. Three of the four returned to full-time pastoral tasks, with a renewed appreciation for the pressures of their congregants. The fourth was inspired to start a business in a challenging neighborhood and remained an elder. We are all full-time for Jesus!

Pastors and spiritual leaders, you have a particular responsibility to commission congregants for all good work and to prayerfully help women and men of all ages be equipped for a new economic era. People are living and working well beyond sixty-five; what does this mean for how we order our lives? Some industries are disappearing while others are emerging. How do we help people develop stability in character and vocation while also remaining flexible about work?

Outcome 25: Insights into Gifts and Talents

One component of Vocational Clarity involves developing understanding of your gifts and talents, strengths and weaknesses. To fully understand my calling and my work, it is important to recognize the spiritual gifts and skill sets God has invested in my life, the skills He expects me to invest in His Kingdom (Rom 12:1-8; 1 Cor 12:18-19).

Understanding our natural and spiritual gifts, personality strengths and weaknesses, and particular aptitudes will help us serve God and others. It is important that we see all of our abilities as gifts from God rather than limiting the idea of "gifts" just to momentary manifestations of the Spirit (1 Cor 12, 14) or "spiritual" assignments and titles (Rom 12; Eph 4:11).

Here is a surprising insight: *God can add gifts and talents over time and has the right to expand and/or narrow our sense of calling.* Some abilities are natural and need cultivation. Others can be learned and refined. For example, some people are born with a beautiful singing voice. Others make a "joyful noise" to the Lord! The singer needs to develop the talent, and the rest of us can learn to sing a bit better but will probably not lead worship or be on a TV talent show! On the other hand, most of us can learn how to manage money, do good research, pray for others diligently, and lead more wisely.

Understanding our specific gifts and talents is never an excuse not to add more skills or humbly serve where needed. One day, a church member was asked to help set up tables and chairs for a church dinner. His reply was, "That is not my calling or ministry." The host immediately looked him in the eyes and said, "Are you too good to serve others, or just self-deceived?" The brother apologized and stared helping. It is right for us to focus our efforts—as well as remain flexible in our families and communities.

I (Charlie) am a solid (neither poor or extraordinary) administrator, and over the decades my leadership roles have demanded my acquiring new skills. I am a better encourager, teacher, convener, and leader, but none of these functions go well without learning administrative skills and new technologies. Spreadsheets, profit and loss statements, and project management guides are all my friends.

As we refine our sense of calling and discover more about our gifts and talents, we discover a "C-4" vision for fruitfulness in God's Kingdom, regardless of our particular assignments:

- The first C is *Character*. Godly character is the foundation and fruit of the Christian life.
- As we grow with our character shaped by holy love,

the second C, *Charisms*, now has a context for flourishing. Charisms are our gifts and talents. There are many extremely gifted women and men who flame out in life and leadership because they have not developed solid character. When we are shaped by the fear of the Lord and faithfulness to truth, then all our gifts can shine, and God will be glorified.

- The third C is *Competencies*—abilities that are both natural and learned. While I (Charlie) am not called or gifted as an accountant, I can develop sufficient competency in reading financial statements and learning from experts when needed. While I am not a doctor, I can learn first-aid and CPR.

- The fourth C is *Capacity*. Jesus declared that we are called to "bear much fruit," and that the fruit of obedient lives would be lasting (John 15:1-11).

We cannot "be anything we want," as some people propose. God has designed the body of Christ to need the uniqueness of each member (1 Cor 12), and God's common grace includes the diverse contributions of all people and the domains of society. Our task is discovering and developing our gifts and talents and becoming the best version of ourselves we can be for God's glory and the good of others.

Outcome 26: Mission with Spouse

My calling is integrally tied to the person with whom God has joined me (Eph 5:22-33; 1 Pet 3:1-7). Our ministries complement one another as we learn to minister in harmony even if we possess different callings.

It is vital to understand singleness as a calling of equal worth as marriage (See Dr. Charlie's "Vocations and Occupations" essay in the Resources section). If you are single, this outcome does not apply. Sometimes singleness is for a season, sometimes for a lifetime. For the women and men who are single: you are NOT incomplete or of lesser status… not are you elevated above others.

In the last chapter we shared some insights about shared mission. Here we will unpack the practical implications of walking in unity with our spouses. This outcome assumes that shared mission includes mutual love and respect. If there are children, this outcome includes their loving and wise nurture as central to the mission, as well as including them in shared activities of the mission.

Marriage changes our world…children change our universe! Some couples cannot have or choose not to have children. This is fine with the Lord, and they can discover and carry out their shared mission. Other couples choose adoption and foster care as central to their calling. The Holy Spirit will direct the path; our task is faithfulness.

Here are five insights that will help couples flourish:

- Mutual love and respect for their different personalities, callings, and gifts. Our spouses are not projects or people that we try to bend toward our ideal—they are unique gifts from God for our world.

- Communicating and praying about shared interests and values. The intersections of a couple's life together serve as the foundation for their shared fruitfulness.

- Desiring the flourishing of our partners and our children above our own.
- Focusing on shared mission aims.
- Contributing and serving together.

A biblical marriage is a wonderful thing, and sometimes it is the place where God brings healing and hope. Long-hidden wounds and deep emotional scars can appear, and the Lord uses our loving spouses to affirm, challenge, and offer hope.

One couple framed their shared mission around orphanages. The husband was a nurse, and the wife was an IT administrator. In their spare time, they contributed financially and strategically to seeing orphan care improve. Their different skills were helpful, and they shared the same heart for the vulnerable. Over a ten-year period, they helped ten orphanages offer better care, streamline administration, and improve communications and funding. They framed their shared mission as, "We Care."

God has a common mission for every family. Discovering the divine pathways will unite spouses and children.

Outcome 27: Teamwork

An important part of vocational clarity is the realization that there are others who have gifts and talents that are meant to augment our calling. I cannot function and thrive alone. I must learn that my calling can only be effective when it is done as part of a team (1 Cor 12, 14).

Everyone says they are a "team player"—until things get tough. Disciples of Jesus do all they can to foster harmony and cooperation and help everyone be heard and improve.

The outcome of teamwork has many applications. In the home, it means mutual decision-making and shared labor. In our churches, this means that lay leaders and staff are all heard, and decisions are made with prayer, not just top-down decrees. In our daily work, it means offering a full day's labor and doing all things with integrity while fitting in well with colleagues.

Teamwork is a term borrowed from sports. Many love their particular teams and some of the superstars connected with them. Here is an interesting fact: the famous players we remember—the Hall of Fame members—all affirm that it took a team for them to shine. The great Michael Jordan needed others to pass and rebound so he could score with spectacular style. Quarterbacks in football need receivers, runners, and linemen to do their jobs well, or their great passes never happen. Goalies in hockey and soccer are rarely remembered like the scorers, but they win as many games for their teams. Even "individual" sports (tennis, track, and others) have coaches, trainers, experts, and others composing a team.

Especially in the highly individualistic culture of the West, teamwork too often takes a back seat to personal achievements and notoriety. We watch as professional agents and scouts talk to twelve- and thirteen-year-old athletes, tempting them with fame while exploiting their potential for fiscal gain. Far too many motivational speakers and courses are designed around personal performance with little regard for others.

God does care about each of us fulfilling our purpose—and this is inseparable for blessing others and helping them use all their gifts as well. As mentioned before, it takes a team for a person to triumph against the odds of poverty, racism, abuse, and marginalization. Second Peter 1:1-4 declares that the Lord has given believers all we need for life and godliness through our knowledge of Him who has called us. Our triune Lord is the ultimate team in our corner, and the body of Christ, local and global, are most often the provisions God gives us for our success.

Outcome 28: Seek the Common Good

The Bible commands believers to love their enemies, pray for those in authority, and do all they can to live at peace with all, as they witness for the Lord (Rom 12-13; 1 Tim 2). Communities need social capital in order to function well. Social capital is the benefit a community receives when individuals and groups cooperate and serve one another. In the absence of social capital, people demand more services from government, and if that is not possible, the community suffers. When we look at the life of Jesus, we see how many times He went about "doing good" (Acts 10:38). He provided food for thousands who were hungry, augmented the wine supply at a wedding, and even healed people who did not even come back to say thank you.

Disciples seek the common good because this is what Jesus would have done.

Revivals are wonderful. When God comes near and helps us be convicted of sin and refreshed in our callings, we rejoice. We should pray for revival—and even more, we should pray and work for an awakening. An awakening is when spiritual renewal of the Church overflows for social transformation. Both are part of God's plan for the world. Please do not separate the joys of conversion from a healthy community.

In the awakenings of the eighteenth and early nineteenth centuries, leaders integrated the call for conversions and spiritual renewal with causes for community and national transformation. Our concerns for economic and social justice, the end of sex and work slavery, better conditions in housing and improvements in education—all of these connect with discipleship.

In the U.S., this inherent integration of salvation and social justice was ripped apart as every Christian tradition separated over race and slavery between the 1820s and 1850s. During the Civil War, each side declared divine blessing! Thankfully, there has been (often slow) progress since the Civil Rights work of the 1960s, but the challenge remains for the Church to demonstrate in practice what she declares from the pulpit. Believers and their local churches must care about both personal salvation and community flourishing if they are going to express the life of Jesus fully.

Stephen Smith was a free African American businessman in nineteenth-century Philadelphia. He was extremely successful, and his racist rivals burned down his businesses! Undeterred, Smith demanded that the city repay much of the rebuilding costs—and they did. Over several decades, Smith created hundreds of jobs, started the first vacation resort open to African Americans, built multiple Underground Railroad locales for slaves seeking freedom, and funded many churches and charities. Amid systemic racism and great opposition, the common good was promoted.

In a recent pastors' conference, I (Jamé) shared that the key to a spiritually thriving and economically sustainable local church was *not* asking, "How do we fund our church and its activities?" The first question should be, "How do we glorify God and bless the zip codes we serve?" Answering the second question results in divine provision for the first one!

One rural pastor asked the Lord to show him how to bless his county. He prayed and listened to leaders around him from all sectors of society. Over a five-year period, his church launched three sustainable preschools, a Christian academy, and other businesses and charities. His church blesses the entire county, and careful stewardship means they are not dependent on weekly offerings for all their expenses.

Outcome 29: Mentoring Others

As disciples grow in maturity, the time comes for them to mentor those who are young in the faith in the development of their callings and skills. This reflects Paul's teaching to Timothy when he encourages him to commit the good news to faithful followers who in turn would be able to teach others (2 Tim 2:2). In this outcome, we ask that you evaluate your capacity and readiness to enter into such a mentorship role.

Disciples make disciples. We are not detailing the particular processes but calling on all believers and their leaders to help Christians be able to share their story and help others on their journey. This is why outcome-based thinking is so important—we mentor others with an end in mind, the fullness and wholeness of Christ in those we serve.

Mentoring others begins with caring and availability, openness to friendship, and a desire for growth. I (Charlie) was the recipient of so much formal (small groups, pastors) and informal (friendships, prayer circles, adults ready to encourage) mentoring in my first few years as a believer. I still mine the riches of all the positive input (and occasionally discarding superfluous ideas as well).

This outcome prompts a special pause for reflection. We are writing this book, and we created the DDA™ (www.discipleshipdynamics.com) as part of a revolution in discipleship and mission that engages "the whole church taking the whole gospel to the whole world."[31] We are not saying that every single Christian must participate in a particular program and care for specific numbers of people. We *are* saying that followers of Jesus should be able to share the

---

31 Christopher Wright helped create this statement in connection with the Lausanne Movement for World Evangelization.

gospel wisely and, in cooperation with their local church, help nurture new and renewed believers. In our churches often a great chasm exists between the hand raised to follow Jesus in a service and mentoring the person who said, "Yes!" to the Lord. We can do better.

The DDA is not a gift discovery test or a skills evaluation. It will give you understanding about your clarity in these areas.

We are all called to the Kingdom and given both universal and specific assignments by the Lord as we join Jesus's redemptive mission. Let's discover and delight in our vocations and occupy well until Jesus comes.

Pray this focusing prayer for vocational clarity:

"Merciful Lord, forgive me for expecting detailed guidance from you without obedience to your clear commands. Help me seek you in prayer and in searching the Scriptures. Help me treat my family members and neighbors with love and kindness. Help me order my loves and refine my thoughts so that agape love rules over my sinful passions. As I seek your glory, please grant understanding of the best ways I can serve you, using your gifts wisely and helping others to do the same. Please grant my family and me a sense of mission that will help focus our time and treasure well. Thank you that I am fearfully and wonderfully made and under your care from conception to coronation. In Jesus's Name, Amen."

For Reflection

1. What do you know about your personality, your natural and spiritual gifts, and your particular sense of calling? How have others affirmed your understanding?

2. How are you honoring God with your daily work (paid or unpaid)? Do you see why it matters?

3. Are you actively mentoring at least one person and open to serve others with what you have learned about God's Kingdom?

DIMENSION FIVE:
Offering All of Daily Life as Worship (Economics and Work)

"PC [Pastor Charlie], My team and I are just as much ministers as you and the church staff. People come to us needing help, and we send them on their way safely. We have to keep up with the latest technology and do our jobs with great care. Families depend on us to get to work and church, vacations and other destinations. We are ministers, too."[32]

"There is a moral case for free markets, rooted in good intentions and sound economics."[33]

"Earn all you can. Save all you can. Give all you can."[34]

It's Sunday night and I'm (Jamé) sending out emails, getting to do lists ready, and prepping for Monday

---

[32] Scotty McVea, founder of Scotty's Automotive in Campbell, CA, conversation with Charlie Self, 2008.

[33] Robert Sirico, *Defending the Free Market: The Moral Case for a Free Economy* (Washington, DC: Regenery Publishing: 2021), 1-8, 25-44. Father Sirico is the founder of the Acton Institute.

[34] Wesley, "Use of Money." Wesley is co-founder of the Methodist movement, and he gave away nearly $5M during his lifetime.

morning. My twenty-something nephew, grinding through an MBA (a Master of Business Administration degree) at a prestigious university, comments, "Uncle Jamé, are you giving people the 'Sunday Scaries'?" I pause. I laugh. Then I reply, "The what?" He says, "the 'Sunday Scaries.'" I reply, "That is …?" "Oh well, that's where you start having anxiety about Monday morning." Ugh. "You know, when people say, 'Time to go to the salt mines' or 'Let's get that bread.'" He was sharing how most people feel about Monday morning work. In contrast to his cynicism and humor, I (Jamé) affirm that our work and participation in the economy matters to our discipleship, because it matters to God (Col 3:17-23).

As we were creating the Discipleship Dynamics assessment, and in our consulting work with focus groups, it is this dimension that always raises eyebrows. It is the one that most people find surprising. Why? Most pastors and church leaders frame discipleship toward making good church volunteers, service attenders, and givers. These are good and important, but only a part of our daily lives.

Remember, our mission with this book and the DDA (www.discipleshipdynamics.com) involves helping to end two big problems in how we think about discipleship and mission. First is the "Sunday-Monday Heresy." Churches must make disciples for Monday, not only Sunday. *Sunday's enthusiasm must become Monday's ethics.* The second is focusing on outcomes and not just outputs. Churches are famous for having lots of outputs such as small groups and classes. Instead, we should be thinking about outcomes. How am I actually applying this sermon on Tuesday at 10:17 a.m.

Dimension 5

while returning emails to people who don't respond? How does God's Word speak to my problems with a fussy baby and a household budget in the red?

In the previous chapter on Vocational Clarity, we indicated that God is vitally interested that we know our general and specific callings in Christ. In this dimension, we affirm that the workplace and participation in the economy is the context where we live out the Great Commission (Matt 28:18-20; Acts 1:8), the Great Commandment (Matt 22:37-40), and our personal mission (Eph 2:10). Work (your business, office, worksite, military installation, or home) is where you impact society, contribute to the common good, and help create a better world. This is your mission field where you function as salt and light to the world.

This is important: *We define work as all meaningful and moral activity apart from leisure or rest.* Paid or volunteer, leadership or labor, home or office, factory or field, we are all called to work. *The economy is human participation the moral and social exchange of goods and services for unlimited wants with limited resources in local and global communities.*

We use a broad and integrative definition of the term *economy* because many disciples work in non-traditional jobs, and many have more than one "gig" going at once. Except for some trades and certain serving professions, staying in one career or job is becoming the exception, not the rule, for many. We are honoring students, persons who volunteer their time for a community service, or household managers who care for children or aging parents, among many other expressions of good work.

When my (Jamé) children were small, I was home two days a week, and that's legitimate work! It made me crazy when people would say, "Oh are you babysitting?" I would respond, "No, I'm parenting." Men parent too.

All these activities are meaningful because they add value to the household economy and the common good. Although the outcomes in this section may appear to be aimed at paid employment, they apply to all categories of work.

We have identified six discipleship outcomes in this dimension.

Outcome 30: Workplace Ethics

Jesus declared that even unbelievers should praise the good works of His followers (Matt 5:13-16). This begins with our work ethics. Businesses, factories, organizations, government offices, police departments, and restaurant chains all have the same challenge: to provide the best services in cost-effective and honest ways. The pressure to "bend the rules" or to use questionable methods to perform our jobs is always present, and we must wage spiritual warfare against those temptations.

Practically, when we talk about work ethics, it shows up in areas like not bending the rules, cutting corners, not shopping on Amazon when you should be working, and treating the company's money like your own money. These are all the temptations we face as real spiritual warfare showing up in the workplace.

When our workplace is unethical and unjust, we are faced

with the decision to stay and change the culture or exit. Jesus says we are "salt" and "light" (Matt 5:13-16), and sometimes we end up in difficult places. As disciples, we must think about our influence in the workplace and how to treat one another, whether we are an employee or an employer. Our influence in workplace ethics is in businesses, factories, organizations, government offices, police departments, and restaurant chains all have the same challenge: to provide the best services in cost-effective and honest ways.

For Christians, workplace ethics means more than rule-keeping and basic honesty. They go deeper into our motives for our work, our attitudes toward co-workers, and our refusal to "play the games" like the political, power-hungry colleagues who often plague our workspaces.

Our workplace ethics are grounded in

- the love command of Jesus (Matt 22:37-40) to honor God supremely and desire the best for our colleagues;
- our desire to offer our work as worship (Rom 12:1-2; Col 3:17-23);
- the fruit of the Spirit (Gal 5:22-23) that express the character of Jesus through us;
- the virtues of our new nature (2 Pet 1:1-10); and
- the good works we do that cause others to notice (Matt 5:13-16).

Years ago, a Kingdom-minded international banker was

arranging a major billion-dollar deal. At the last minute, a key administrator suddenly demanded an extra $250,000 "special fee." In other words, a bribe. The banker refused, the deal broke down, and he went back home in disgrace, for he did not publicly expose the unethical person. At the corporate office, the Vice President walked in, and everyone expected the architect of the failed deal to get fired. As the VP walked into the main office, he called out in a loud voice, "Where is my honest banker?" Instead of being sacked, the ethical banker was promoted!

Sometimes our love for the Lord will demand that we expose immoral behavior and unjust systems. Throughout history, Christians have led the way in transforming society, including the workplace. From abolition of slavery to improving factory conditions, from child labor to organizing farm workers, believers have affirmed that free markets and the common good can unite. Everyone benefits when righteousness and justice meet (Ps 85:10-13). With humility and a concern for all, believers must serve as beacons for their fellow-workers.

We cannot promise that integrity will always be rewarded immediately, but in the long run of eternity and time, the influence of good ethics has a positive ripple effect in the economy and in many lives.

Outcome 31: Mission at Work

The second outcome in this dimension reflects your sense of mission at work. Your workplace is the field into which you have been sent to labor (Matt 9:37-10:1). Let that sink in for a little bit: God has called you a partner in His mission where you work. This is the context to which God has called you and where you can bring a sense of His presence to the people with whom you work. Believers are not wholly defined by their jobs; however, we believe that we can bring a sense of calling to the workplace.

If we were to ask the simple question, "Why do we work?" then the most basic of responses would be, "For money." This is probably the worst answer, though. Colossians 3:23 states, "Whatever you do, do your work heartily, as for the Lord and not for people" (NASB). When we work, we are working as worship to God. This matters in our discipleship because when we work, we are doing two things simultaneously: worshiping the Lord and creating value for God's world at the same time.

The Old Testament Hebrew language offers a rich picture of this integration. Work and worship are united in the Hebrew word *avodah*. First, this word means work in contexts, such as "there was no man to *work* the ground" (Gen 2:5) and God's command to Adam concerning the Garden to "*work* it and take care of it" (Gen 2:15). In strict linguistic terms, when we work, we are creating value. So, we work, and we produce something.

Avodah can also mean worship. "This is what the LORD says: Let my people go, so that they may *worship [avodah]* me" (Exod 8:1). This indicates that our work may be seen as worship if we offer it to God. Business is the way we organize our work, the abilities and energies of others, and available resources. When submitted to God, our work becomes an act of worship. This is what the Apostle Paul means when he says for believers (in response to God's grace in Christ), to offer their bodies (their whole selves) to God as an act of spiritual worship! (Rom 12:1-2).

Mark Green, former leader of the London Institute for Contemporary Christianity and a leader in the global faith and work movement, calls our daily work assignments God's "frontline" in mission. We are praying for colleagues, family members, and neighbors. We are doing our work for God's glory, and we are looking for divine appointments for sharing the gospel.

Michael Thigpen, an Old Testament scholar and seminary leader, worked at a bank during his grueling years of graduate study. During those years, he hated his job most of the time and longed for graduation and the beginning of his "real" work. By his admission, he was stuck in the sacred/secular dichotomy; today, he wishes he had embraced that experience much more. Positively, Michael speaks about the goodness of all moral work in Genesis 1-2 and how even the fall of humankind in Genesis 3 does not eradicate the original divine mandate.

God often calls believers to hard places, to refine our character, to witness for Jesus and justice, and to see changes in us and in those around us. It is often difficult knowing how God is working when our work is repetitive, tough, and not what we desire. It is helpful remembering that most of the hearers and readers of the Bible had no choices concerning their class or locale, career or even choice of spouse!

Dimension 5

Outcome 32:
Understand Your Contribution to the Economy

To be a channel of God's wisdom and grace to your workplace requires having a good understanding of the field(s) in which you function. You should become knowledgeable about the changes taking place, the challenges your workplace faces, and how to increase the competitive advantage of your products and services. You should also know how your work creates value in people's lives, whether increasing efficiency, encouraging creative thinking, or simply bringing delight through wholesome expressions of creativity. This is as true for the person making pizzas as it is for the computer programmer.

Our audiences, students, and clients continually ask us, "What is economics?" Economics is not only about money but about exchange and value creation; it involves collective human behavior measured in empirical knowledge (data and statistics rightly interpreted!). For example, consider an accountant and a plumber. The accountant has sprung a leak with water running all over the bathroom, so she hires a plumber. The plumber needs help running the business because he has too much work, so he hires an accountant to do that for him. The accountant and the plumber both exchange services with each other and it is regulated through a price. The plumber and the accountant function in different fields of work, but they pay one another for the expertise. Plus, we guarantee you that often the plumber is more expensive than the accountant!

Being a channel of God's wisdom and grace in your

workplace includes having a good understanding of how your participation in the economy benefits others while simultaneously benefiting yourself. There are many (at least eleven by some counts) sectors in the economy, and they change all the time. These changes create competitive advantages or destabilize industries. As a disciple, it is important that we know how we add value to our domains and how we create value in people's lives. Of course, we need to earn money, but this is a fruit of the value we create.

The terms *entrepreneur* and *entrepreneurial* are used often in many faith and work circles. In today's 'gig' economy with many working multiple jobs, understanding our calling is important. Not everyone is called and equipped to start a business. However, we are all "God's contractors" to every job we have, aiming to please God and serve well. We are all stewards of God's grace and gifts and commanded to manage ourselves and our households well.

Johan and I (Charlie) were at a conference in Phoenix, AZ years ago, enjoying the balmy weather of a winter day in the desert. Our hotel restaurant had pleasant outdoor dining, and our table was served by a joyful team member who obviously loved her job. She took all orders without a single written note, kept water glasses full, and brought the food to each person efficiently and with a flourish. Johan declared to her, "It looks like you are enjoying your job too much!" She laughed and said that she took pride in her work and in giving her customers a positive experience. The people at the table paused and reflected on her positive attitude (we were at a faith and work conference!), and a spirit of humility overtook us all as we renewed our own attitudes that day.

A thoughtful person may ask, "Value? How does that work when I feel like my job is meaningless?" We may think we have a no-name job just working for a paycheck, but the simplest tasks are part of what the Rev. Dr. Martin Luther King called, "the web of mutuality." Here are his eloquent words dignifying all our labor: "In a real sense all life is inter-related. All men are caught in an inescapable network of mutuality, tied in a single garment of destiny. Whatever affects one directly, affects all indirectly. I can never be what I ought to be until you are what you ought to be, and you can never be what you ought to be until I am what I ought to be…This is the inter-related structure of reality."[35]

King was referring not just to economics but all our social interactions. In his quest for justice, he encouraged street-sweepers that they mattered just as much as the famous playwright, Shakespeare. There are "no little people,"[36] and as along as the work is moral, no unimportant jobs.

Outcome 33: Creativity and Innovation

I (Jamé) often think of God as the first entrepreneur. In

---

35 Martin Luther King Jr., "Letter from A Birmingham Jail," Good Reads, accessed June 29, 2022, https://www.goodreads.com/quotes/432654-in-a-real-sense-all-life-is-inter-related-all-men.

36 Francis Schaeffer, *No Little People, with a New Introduction by Udo W. Middelmann* (Crossway: 2021). This is the title and theme of the entire book.

Genesis 1 and 2 we see that He literally took nothing and created something creative and innovative (the entire cosmos, our planet, and a garden)! Likewise, I think of Adam and Eve in the Garden who were just given the raw materials. There was no bread, no fire, no shelter in the original Garden of Eden. In fact, there is a bit of wistfulness before our first parents emerged: "There was no one to work the ground…" (Gen 2:5). Even before sin came into the world, God created the opportunity for human creativity and innovation. Our work is our garden!

Creativity is not confined to actors, writers, musicians, dancers, painters, sculptors, or a few entrepreneurs. Creativity can apply to new ways of seeing how to manage a work process, or original thinking about a ministry. Innovation is quite similar: the focus here is fresh thinking on current products and processes. Here are some examples drawn from our experiences and research:

- A line worker in a factory sees a better way to improve efficiency and quality.
- A waiter discovers a way to arrange tables and timetables for better service.
- The late Steve Jobs' brilliance at Apple Computer was to begin with the customer experience and then design the technology to that end.
- Musical genius includes integrating multiple types of music in a song or album, appealing to many ages and cultures.

How can we be creative, regardless of our work? First, our spiritual gifts do not stop when we leave church. The Holy

Spirit is with us 24/7. When we are at work, both natural and spiritual gifts integrate. As a disciple, you become a conduit of God's grace in that economic context. The Holy Spirit can give you insights (Eph 3:14-21; Phil 1:9-10) into better ways of doing the work, quicker ways of processing materials, more efficient methods, or better strategies of organization. There are numerous ways that we can bless our workplaces.

It is right that we ask the Holy Spirit to lead, guide, and bring wisdom (Prov 2-3; 1 Cor 2; Jas 1:5; 3:17-19) to our daily tasks.

Outcome 34: Asset to My Work Colleagues

As we do our work unto the Lord (Eph 6:5-9; Col 3:23-24), God wants us to be an asset to our colleagues at work. The way we do our work, the way we interact with our colleagues, and our commitment to excellence all serve as important elements in our discipleship process. Our presence should bring a sense of God's peace to the workplace.

Do we know the difference between an asset and a liability? An asset brings value and/or makes you money. A liability undermines value and costs money and time. When you work, you are either an asset or a liability. All disciples should be assets in places of work, whether at home, volunteering, or doing paid work. As we do our work for the Lord (Eph 6:5-9; Col 3:23-24), God wants us to function as assets. The way we do our work, how we treat people, and our commitment to the mission of enterprises are all important ingredients of being a follower of Jesus. We must discard the idea that work is just a curse and money some kind of "filthy lucre" (1 Tim 3:3, KJV). When we work, we work unto the Lord. When we cash our paychecks, we create value for our families, our church, and our communities.

Remember, most of us spend most of our waking hours working! Therefore, this is important to God. The relationships we have at work matter. We do not worship the almighty dollar but the Almighty God. Everyone is made in the image of God; therefore, everyone is worthy of love and dignity because they reflect the very nature and creativity of God. Our witness and how we love our life at work publicly reflect the private work of the Holy Spirit in us. Whatever is inside of us eventually comes out publicly. If we hate our job and hate the people around us, that attitude will come out and not be good. As disciples, we have choices that help us control our attitudes and actions so we can love even the 'unlovable' with whom we serve. Sometimes we may need to leave self-destructive or unjust places, but only after prayer and efforts to shine for Christ.

Remember group projects in elementary and secondary school? They always seemed to include three types of participants: the natural leader, the slacker, and those along for the ride! God calls every believer to offer their best at every task, contributing to the whole. Whether we lead or follow, we offer our best. And yes, it feels frustrating sometimes when others let us carry the weight. However, we are working for the Lord (Col 3:17-23) and not just showing off for the boss.

Dimension 5

Our presence should be a like a bright shining light where people feel drawn to us and desire to work with us because of the love of Christ. Remember, Jesus says people will know we are His disciples by the way we love one another (John 13:35; 2 Cor 5:14; 1 John 4:7-8).

Outcome 35: Stewards of the Environment

When we start talking about the environment, some wonderful disciples urgently plea, "In ten years, it will be too late! The earth will be destroyed by climate change!" Other disciples on the other side exclaim, "Well, I don't believe in global warming; that's a bunch of globalist nonsense!"

Can we just take a breath and calm down for a second? Let's frame this biblically: Where is our garden? Our local garden is everywhere we live, play, and work, and it is connected to the whole earth. We see this in Scripture as we realize that God created the earth in all its magnificent beauty and gave Adam and Eve the task of managing its diversity and caring for its bounty (Gen 1-2; Ps. 8).

David made sure we understood that the earth belongs to the Lord, including everything that is in it (Ps 24:1). This was such an important verse that Paul decided to quote David to reinforce its importance (1 Cor 10:26). *Spirit-empowered disciples take care of the environment because it is the handiwork of our God.* It is also a sign of the coming Kingdom, when the earth and the heavens will be renewed completely, and we will worship and work in perfect harmony. The Holy Spirit in us is the "down payment" (Eph 1:14) of our future; therefore, when we care for creation, it is a sign of the future to all around us.

Please, let's hear this in our spirits today: the eternal Kingdom we look forward to will include a real earth with the redeemed people of God worshiping and working in real bodies. Our Lord Jesus Christ rose from the dead in a transformed body that was healed, whole, and tangible, even enjoying a breakfast of fish by the seashore! (John 21). When we see our risen Lord, we see a preview of our future. Therefore, all we do today by the power of the Spirit is not merely temporal labor but a foretaste of the future.

When God breathed on Adam and Eve, they were the crowning work of His creation. Sometimes as disciples we miss this point—that every person we come in contact with, is made in the image of God and connected to the creative nature of who God is. When we say we care for the creation, that does not only mean good stewardship of the natural resources but also caring for every person, because they bear God's image and are worth the blood of Christ shed on the Cross. We do not worship creation. We worship the Creator. Therefore, creation care is an act of worship as we steward all God has entrusted to humankind.

Christians have very diverse opinions on the politics of climate change and the environment. Creation care is ultimately part of God's work of justice in the world, for most who suffer from environmental degradations are the poor. As we care for God's world, more people will flourish economically, physically, and even spiritually as they see the Creator's goodness in our wise stewardship. Good ecological policies are good for long-term economic growth.

When we were children, the Great Lakes of North America were extremely polluted. Today, they are places for both industry and recreation. Care for God's world is vital for sustainable economic flourishing.

We have limited time because one day, the Kingdom will fully come, and we will have new heavens and new earth (Rev 21:1-6). In other words, we are looking forward to a second creation story where disciples will simultaneously worship and work in the age to come. What we do now with the stewardship of creation will matter for today and forever. In the Old Testament, the Holy Spirit came upon the people of God for a sense of mission, but in the New Testament the Holy Spirit is now within believers to empower them to do the work set before them. The Holy Spirit now is in the "down payment" (2 Cor 5:5) of our future; therefore, when we care for creation, it is a sign of the future kingdom for believers and a watching world.

Pray this focusing prayer for economics and work:

"Loving Lord, you have created a bountiful world with enough for all to flourish. Forgive our idolatry of materialism, our immorality of self-centeredness, and the injustice of allowing systemic evil to keep others from thriving. We offer our heads, hearts, and hands to you as we go to work. Help us reform and transform where we can, aiming for the good of all. Help us act and speak with integrity. Empower creativity, and may we be attentive to your voice as we labor each day. May we bring foretastes of your Kingdom future as we care for your world and one another. In Jesus's Name, Amen."

For Reflection

1. How do others see you at your workplace? Are you a source of encouragement? Are your ethics and habits inspiring or mediocre?

2. How are you caring for the environment?

3. How does your daily work make the world a better place?

CONCLUSION
The Path Forward: Envision, Equip, and Assess

What a wonderful life God has designed for every believer and each community! If you have read through this book, you are probably both blessed and a bit overwhelmed. You cannot retreat to traditional activities, yet this vision of discipleship confronts us with a decision: will we go forward in faith, focus our attention on pleasing God and serving others, and follow-through with first steps of obedience? Or will we remain in a wilderness of frustration?

A leader at one of our events exclaimed, "This is work! I was hoping for a simple 'how to' on making disciples and maybe a video series. Y'all are asking my team and I to do a lot."

Yes.

Lasting change, including character and community transformation, cannot be packaged into a tidy program. *Dimensional, outcome-based discipleship will, however, make many tasks more efficient and effective and help create a culture of self-feeding, a conversation all ages can share, and even change how we share our faith.* For example,

- This vision ends the sacred-secular dichotomy, with all believers empowered for mission through any and every placement. Those called to

- missionary service and spiritual leadership recognize their holy duty to equip God's people for mission in all of life.

- The Five Dimensions can also become a witnessing tool, as we ask pre-believers real-life questions, such as, "Are you in awe of the universe?" or "Would you like to be whole inside, free from your history and filled with hope?" or "How are your relationships?" or "Do you have a sense of purpose when you wake up each day?" and "Do you know how important your work is to the world?"

- As mentioned, the dimensions and outcomes offer every community the foundation for a cohesive, unifying conversation. Small groups are energized as these are used to check in and encourage one another. Families can share around the dinner table. Children's and student ministries are transformed with a clear template for maturing children into adult believers.

- This vision compels dependency on the Holy Spirit and listening to our congregations, organizations, and communities. As Jamé shared in chapter five on the topic of economics and work, sustainable households, churches, and organizations are solving challenges in their zip codes and helping others flourish.

- Johan offered tremendous wisdom on personal wholeness; we need this in our broken world! All of us are carrying baggage we need to release. Some also carry the deep wounds of abuse and rejection, confusion on identity and purpose, and a sense of hopelessness. We do recommend professional help for persistent emotional and mental needs. Counselors we consulted for this book also affirmed that friendships are vital to health and that some afflictions find healing in community.

- To get practical for pastors: if you combine your unique way of sharing these dimensions with the DDA tool for your community, your preaching calendar emerges quickly, your small group structure is transformed, and more people will become part of your team because you have endorsed and empowered their everyday life as vital to God's mission. The more we affirm the importance of all good work, the more margin people will have to participate in church initiatives!

Three Keys to Unlock This New Vision

Envision: We must "see" the flourishing life Jesus intends for all of us (John 10:10) and embrace God's will with faith.

Equip: As we envision wholeness in Christ, we can equip one another with the abundant resources the Lord has provided, organizing them around the Five Dimensions and thirty-five outcomes of the assessment.

Assess: We need to measure and celebrate progress as well as face issues that need work in our lives. This is why we created the DDA (www.discipleshipdynamics.com) to encourage progress.

Back to our couple, Julie and Rob. The Five Dimensions are helping them order their days, strengthen their marriage, and manage the "crazy" that everyday circumstances bring to all families. They are learning to listen to God and pray all day. Bible passages and verses become points of reflection during work. Their interactions are both bolder and kinder. They are starting to sketch a mission for their family. Their economy has always been OK, but now they are thinking about increasing both their earning power and generosity.

The heart of this book and this vision is "seeing" the goal of all our desires and disciplines: God's glory, the good of others. Our personal wholeness and social flourishing are the fruit of this integrity and intentionality. We were created—and redeemed—to enjoy God and engage in the work He offers as we walk with Him.

AFTERWORD

Scott Hagan, PhD
Former President of North Central University, Minneapolis, MN
Author: *The Language of Influence and Personal Power*
and the *Influential Disciple*

For over three decades, my wife Karen and I have been honored to help plant and lead local churches, author books and training materials, and participate in significant kingdom initiatives. We have had the honor of leading North Central University into a new future. We have learned from many wise women and men, and we have aimed to encourage and equip our congregants, students, and fellow followers of Jesus with the best insights and practices possible for their callings and the mission we share: seeing Jesus transform every neighborhood and nation.

One of our deep burdens is seeing healthier disciples and leaders developed by our local churches, ministries, and schools. Much good is being done, but often disciple-making is reduced to a program or set of practices. If recent research is true, we are not doing well.

In our journey we have been blessed with the influences of the authors of this book. Dr. Charlie Self has been an inspiration for decades as a thought leader, and in the last several years our friendship has deepened. Today, we are partnering on strategic initiatives together. Rev. Jamé Bolds has been a friend for years, and our lives have intersected pastorally and strategically for nearly two decades. Jamé is a brilliant thinker and practitioner, challenging the local church to a new economy that transforms persons and zip codes. We have known Dr. Johan Mostert from his incredible work for justice and community health as he integrates sound theology and the best psychological resources so all can flourish.

This is a powerful team, and this book and the assessment on which it is based are revolutionary tools for transforming how we understand discipleship and mission in the twenty-first century. I urge serious Christians of every vocation and occupation to buy several copies and begin framing your efforts in terms of dimensions and outcomes, instead of starting with programs. I can speak from experience: our churches and ministries did discipleship well, but we would have been more effective with many fewer mistakes if we had the perspectives and resources in this book.

I appreciate the wholeness here, from spiritual intimacy to managing emotions, from loving others deeply and wisely to discerning our calling. And the authors remind us that all the transforming work of God in us and through us takes place as we wake up and work each day. We will be using the insights of this book to help our North Central University community grow in wholeness. When we unite the wisdom of this book with the unique ethos of our missions, fruitfulness grows and our impact increases.

Friends, let's get to work with others re-envisioning discipleship and mission in your life, your church, and for the flourishing of your community.

Resources

The essays and guides in this section are designed to jump-start individuals and groups for forward momentum. There are several overlapping ideas between these works and the content of the book. Our aim is to help as many people as possible apply the insights we have gathered from so many wonderful leaders.

Reimaging Discipleship and Mission for a New Era (Spring 2022)

An Essay by Dr. Charlie Self

These seven insights are gleaned from global leaders and can help us as we look across the street. They are presented in a forward-thinking, "From…To" style that is not a repudiation of the past, but a reconsideration of our future. With the help of the Holy Spirit, we can be faithful to the unchanging truth of the gospel and responsive to the changing spiritual and social landscape. Each insight is followed by an application question.

Insight One: Preserving and Prophesying Truth

The world around us is changing rapidly. The truth of the gospel and the authority of Scriptures offer assurance and stability when everything seems up for grabs. In fact, contending for, "the faith once entrusted to all of God's holy people" (Jude 3) and applying that faith toward serious issues of love and justice, and personal and community wholeness should become a new normal. We need poets and prophets: women and men who will remind us of the unchanging ways of God (poets) and help us confront our need for repentance and renewal (prophets) as we apply truth in our world.

Because our Lord is, "the same yesterday, today, and forever" (Heb 13), and because we worship a loving Father of lights in whom there is no shadow of change (Jas 1), we can have the courage and humility to repair what is broken. Let us winsomely uphold truth and wisely innovate in our expressions of mission.

Application Question: Are we creating a safe place for exploration, hard questions, and maturing in our thinking?

Insight Two: From Game Day to Everyday

Our gatherings for worship and learning, encouragement and empowerment do matter (Heb 10:25). Too often, however, we have made these the supreme focus of our budgets, energies, and other resources, to the detriment of discipleship and mission.

While retaining the importance of worship around God's Word and His Table, this moment offers the chance to invest in other ways of equipping and mission. Our budgets are theological statements. Are we investing in the community as well as communion? Are we serving our members and neighbors with practical resources as well as excellent proclamation?

Application Question: Are we helping people apply truth in everyday living, realizing that daily work is the context for character growth and mission?

Insight Three: From Flaming out to Faithful Presence—Flourishing Leaders

In listening to pastors across the country, we hear this refrain often: "I love the Lord. I know he is with us. My family is OK and I think our church is weathering this moment pretty well. But I am SO tired." Being a spiritual leader is challenging on a good day, let alone in a pandemic and during profound ecclesial and social change! Thankfully, the Lord has provided all we need for an integral life of work, rest, and play, for personal and family wholeness, and fruitfulness in leadership. Self-care is not selfish, and biblical self-denial is not self-destruction.

For years, Dr. Luke Bobo has been sharing insights with leaders on sustainable ministry. As he listens to the stories of women and men called by God yet burning out, he is diligently encouraging these dedicated leaders to take care of their bodies and souls. This includes one's devotional life, peer friendships, professional help if needed. It means realigning expectations so that endurance is not exhaustion and perseverance is not privation. God cares about our whole selves, and healthy leaders will lead healthier communities.

Application Question: Are we working with family, friends, peers, and professionals to create healthy personal rhythms?

Insight Four: From Programs to Outcomes

Fellow-servants, we measure what matters to us. Attendance, offerings, volunteers, participation—all are signs of health. Please notice that these are all *quantitative* metrics. What about knowing the *qualitative* condition of the members and their growth in holy love, hopefulness, and connecting Sunday's experience with Monday's ethics? The American Church has a feast table of resources for maturity in all dimensions of life, yet we have emaciated believers malnourished and needing much help in even basic disciplines. Here is the revolution in discipleship: *we must articulate biblical outcomes reflecting wholeness and have our programs serve these outcomes!* Let's begin a conversation on what maturity looks like on Monday and connect it with our mission. Then we will be embarking on a new pathway of progress. Here is a great tool for this: www.discipleshipdynamics.com.

Application Question: Are we connecting our mission, vision, and values to outcomes for everyday life?

Insight Five: From Offerings to Multiple Income Streams—A New Economy

Cheerful cynics from all walks of life have said, "Vision is spelled M-O-N-E-Y." Economic realities deeply affect our ministries, and so sustaining our local church mission is more challenging every day. Yes, we must encourage God's people in faithful giving and steward such generosity well. It does take a long time for new believers/members to give consistently. Praise God for the women and men of generosity and sacrifice; their efforts will always matter at every level.

This moment of economic struggle is a time for circumspection and creativity leading to sustainable prosperity. Two keys exist for unlocking expanded resources. The first is *thinking about our community flourishing before our own survival*. The second is *commissioning the creativity of our congregants for leading in spiritual and social renewal*. When we face upward and outward, the Lord will then reveal the second key: new revenue streams and structures that will lead to generational stability and continual dependence on the Lord. Offering valuable services, incubating businesses, creating endowments, and other fresh expressions will help make the mission less dependent on the weekly offering.

Application Question: Are we exploring multiple revenue streams and inviting the creativity of our members and network into our planning?

Insight Six: From Institutional Preservation to Community Impact

William Temple, an Anglican Archbishop in the mid-twentieth century, offered these profound words: "The church exists primarily for those who are still outside it."[37] In moments of crisis, it is easy to turn in on ourselves and think about self-preservation. God's pathway in such moments is just the opposite: the more we seek God's glory and the good of others and consider how to unleash every believer for effective witness outside our gatherings, the stronger we will be as a local church!

What if all our members saw their daily work as vital to God's mission? Are we commissioning new businesses and volunteers who work outside our programs as well as clergy and missionaries we sponsor from within? Are we waiting on the Holy Spirit for creativity for what initiatives we lead and where we can collaborate with other churches and groups for the common good? Here is this Kingdom paradox in practical terms: the more we bless the scattered work of the people of God, the more they will have the emotional and spiritual margin to help with specific church programs.

Application Question: Are we listening to the Spirit through the voices of the community and discerning our fields of creativity and collaboration?

Insight Seven: From Reaction to Anticipation

The church, like many other institutions, often finds itself catching up to cultural and social change. Traditionalism

---

37 Archbishop William Temple, recalled as a personal dictum in "Letter from the Archbishop of the West Indies" in *Theology* 59 (1956): n.p. Oxford Reference, accessed June 28, 2022, https://www.oxfordreference.com/view/10.1093/acref/9780191826719.001.0001/q-oro-ed4-00010671.

and trendiness are two unhealthy ways of staying relevant. The good news of Scripture is that God's people have the Holy Spirit; thus, we can understand the times and know God's will (Eph 5:10-17). Humility and openness remain vital, for we have a propensity for denial and even self-deception. It is difficult confronting so much change as we mourn the loss of yesterday's familiarity. Through careful study of the Word and listening to wise voices of common grace in all domains, we can position ourselves as communities of anticipation instead of reaction.

We are also able to bring the lessons of history into our context and unite timeless principles with timely challenges. We are liberated from the fog of nostalgia and the blinding images of "the new." It is more important that we are people of prayer, with all congregants learning more about intercession and the community, devoting time to listening to God together and then partnering with the Spirit as we pray for the salvation of our neighbors and the shalom of our community.

Application Question: Are we in a posture of intercession, receiving the heart and mind of Christ for our mission?

We serve a loving Lord who is working in all circumstances for the good of His people and the reconciliation of the world (Rom 8:28-39; 2 Cor 5:18-6:2). May the Lord help us listen deeply, act decisively, and be a blessing for His glory.

Making Healthy Disciples: A Guide for Leaders

Dear Fellow Leader,

We have unprecedented resources for spiritual and personal growth, yet the challenges are still daunting: hurting people, broken families, and people struggling to connect our faith to daily life. All of us as leaders desire maturity, stability, wholeness, and a sense of purpose in our fellow believers.

The Discipleship Dynamics Assessment (DDA) offers a new vision and process for disciple-making by focusing on OUTCOMES and seeing the Christian life as DIMENSIONAL rather than a linear process of classes or programs.

In addition to offering an eight- to ten-page personal report to all participants, *the DDA offers the leader a dashboard of the average group results, while all personal results remain confidential.* When the leader buys a certain number of assessments and invites people to participate, the dashboard is filled with important data as people complete their surveys. This includes average summary scores in the Five Dimensions *and* average group scores in each of the thirty-five outcomes. Here is an example from one local church with about 150 in attendance:

- Spiritual Formation: 57 percent
- Personal Wholeness: 62 percent
- Healthy Relationships: 54 percent
- Vocational Clarity: 67 percent
- Economics and Work: 72 percent

The pastor noticed that Spiritual Formation, and especially

Life in 5D

Resources

First Steps to Transformation

Assuming that the church/organization is hospitable and integrating new constituents, here are the practical steps that will transform the disciple-making process and integrate the Discipleship Dynamics Assessment™ into the life of the church/organization:

- *Examine the DNA (or "ethos" or "culture") of your church*: your mission, vision, and value statements.

- *Create outcomes that connect real life with the key ideas that God has given that define your identity and mission.* For example, if one of your goals is reaching out to the community, then two outcomes would be "*that every member can share the gospel wisely*" and that they "*care for the marginalized.*" If one of your values is spiritual maturity, then define this in ways that are understandable and measurable as a discipleship outcome—"*pray without ceasing,*" "*love the Word of God,*" and "*pursue biblical principles for living.*"

- *Connect the ethos of your church or organization with the outcomes of the Discipleship Dynamics Assessment (DDA).* (Our team will be available to help if that is needed.)

- Have your *leadership teams take the DDA* and use your dashboard scores (group averages) and enjoy a robust conversation on the best ways to engage the congregation.

- *Prepare a plan so that an adequate percentage of members take the DDA* and plan for an annual retake. (Each individual can take their assessment a second time for free). The assessment is best done with at least a nine- to twelve-month period for learning in between. You will see real progress if you have remained intentional about your work.

Here are some guidelines on how to choose a representative sample of people from the congregation to provide you with an accurate picture of the discipleship status of the entire group:

- We recommend the highest possible percentage of participants from the congregation to be part of your sample. This will increase the *accuracy* and *quality* of your feedback and reduce the margin of error.

- The more people you involve, the more members will have access to their personal results!

- You will want to choose a representative number of persons in each of your congregation's age, gender, culture and/or race groups. In other words, if 60 percent of your congregation is over the age of fifty, then 60 percent of your sample group should also be over the age of fifty.

- Here are some guidelines for minimal participation. For a church or organization with the number of members in the first column, the participants should be the number in the second column:

Number of (Adult) Members	Participants Needed
50	30
100	60
200	100
300	120
400	140
500	150
800	165
1,000	175
5,000	200

Some Guidelines as You Implement This Strategy

Avoid the sacred/secular divide (SSD): Affirm a deep connection between worship and work, devotion and service! All good work is pleasing to God. The Five Dimensions and thirty-five outcomes reinforce that all believers are called to work in the Kingdom, they all have the Holy Spirit, and they are all divinely placed by God in their daily situations.

Share a *sermon series or series of seminars/learning experiences* that offer a fresh vision of outcome-based discipleship, affirming that the DDA is *not* a spiritual report card, but a snapshot of self-understanding!

After you obtain your dashboard results, make sure to share both the strengths and areas for improvement with the leadership and the congregation. Invite those stronger in some outcomes (scores in the 60s and above) to be ready to help others.

- *Be ready to respond to concerns, questions, and surprises!* And note that the scoring is 0-100, with most people having scores from the 40s to the 60s. This is *not* an academic score, like papers in college! Even seasoned leaders will have scores that reflect areas of needed growth. Here is a summary of the score breakdowns used in the assessment:

    - 0-25: This is a new area or one of real struggle for this disciple.

    - 25-50: This is an area where development is in its beginning stages and need to be nurtured.

    - 51-75: This score indicates the disciple is gaining a firm grip on this outcome while they still indicate that they have room to grow in this area.

    - 75-100: The disciple is mature and can help others.

- *Take time to survey members* and find out areas of expertise and experience, passion and placement, giftings and desires. The DDA can provide powerful personal data serving the mission".

- *Develop new resources* for a new culture of empowerment: website, book table, small groups, classes (virtual and live), and other creative ideas that can inform everyone on aspects of the thirty-five outcomes.

- *God's people are MORE capable* than what we give them credit for.

This is a revolution in discipleship—seeing life as dimensional and channeling all our resources toward biblical outcomes.

Using the DDA as a Mentor or Counselor

Professional counselors are familiar with a variety of assessment instruments that they use in their practice. This includes personality tests like the MBTI™, or pathology measures like the Beck Depression Scales, or even interest inventories like the ASVAB™ (Armed Services Vocational Aptitude Battery). What makes these assessments valuable is that they have good psychometric properties, that is, they have validity and reliability. The DDA is proud of its psychometric properties, and we have included a report on our statistics on the website.

While the DDA shares these properties with other personality instruments, it is different in that it remains a confidential assessment, and the scores are not revealed to the counselor or mentor unless the individual has the confidence to share them during the counseling sessions.

When a counselor or mentor decides that a discipleship assessment would be appropriate for their sessions, he or she would direct the person to the website and ask them to complete the DDA.

At the next session, the disciple would bring their confidential assessment with them and begin the discussion of their road to healthy discipleship.

1. Ask them to identify their five strongest outcomes, and rejoice with them at their achievements

2. Ask them to identify one of the lower outcome scores that they would like to discuss.

3. Spend time with them in the Scriptures and engage them to see how this impacts their Christian witness. We also have a list of books we feel can prove helpful to assist in this journey.

4. Between your sessions, give them homework to read, study, and meditate on the identified outcome until they can understand how they need to discipline themselves to achieve that outcome in their daily life.

5. Progress as fast as the context allows to deal with more outcomes.

6. After a period of growth and development, you can ask them to return to the website and take the free, re-assessment. The re-assessment will give the new scores and compare them with the ones they initially received. At this point, you may find that some other scores are now in need of attention, and that your counselee has new strong points. Discipleship is a dynamic process that requires us to constantly adapt our responses to changing life circumstances. This is how you can help the body of Christ to show what "walking in the Spirit" (Gal 5:16-26) is actually all about!

Using the DDA as a Group Leader

The DDA provides group leaders with a unique opportunity to schedule the content of a discipleship growth group in a way that perfectly adapts to the specific, identified needs of that group. While there are many books and curricula for group use on the market today, they all have one thing in common. They are written on a topic that someone must decide is the topic of interest or concern for their specific group. This is not necessarily bad, but you are sure to find that there are times when the curriculum or the chapter under discussion is not relevant for some part of the group, and that this could result in members becoming less engaged.

The DDA, however, provides you with a report on the specific growth needs that your entire group has identified. This increases the possibility that individual members of the group will remain engaged. They know they have had an opportunity to confidentially provide their group leader with the information that he or she needs to develop a curriculum sure to benefit their personal discipleship journey.

Because the DDA remains confidential, a group leader never receives the scores of a group member. When you establish a group, you will get access to the DDA dashboard that gives the average scores of the entire group on each of the Five Dimensions and all thirty-five discipleship outcomes. This is a treasure trove of valuable information and will allow you to tailor your group's sessions around the average scores as specifically identified by your group! When you launch the sessions, group members can be presented with the group's average scores and can compare their private, confidential score with that of the whole group. This is already a potential source of valuable information for the member. How do my scores compare to those of my group? In what way does it appear that I can be a source of help to others who have lower scores than mine? What can I learn from others who feel more confident in this discipleship outcome?

Here are the steps that a group leader takes to incorporate the DDA into their curriculum planning:

1. As the leader, you go online and register yourself the same way any individual would register, with your own email and password. This will take you to your own Discipleship Dynamics home page. We have an entire help file to assist you in the technical aspects of creating a group and distributing the group link to individuals.

2. When your group is taking the assessment, your dashboard will allow you to monitor how many have begun the assessment, how many have finished, and how many still need to complete the work. You can send them a reminder to finish the assessment before a specific date, which you have determined to enable you to start work on analyzing the average group scores.

3. Your group leader dashboard will provide you with the average scores of all participants in all Five Dimensions and the thirty-five outcomes. You will

be able to identify the outcomes that are the strong suit of the group, and these should be celebrated together. You can also identify the outcomes that drew the lowest scores. These are the ones that will need your attention to prepare material and discussion points for the coming sessions.

4. Now you can schedule the sessions for the group. In your planning, create time to celebrate the strong outcomes from the group. Second, decide how long you will spend with the outcomes that need attention. Finally, be sure to allow time at the end for the group to take their second, free assessment. The results of the "posttest" could elicit significant further discussions.

5. You are now in a position to inform the group of the agenda for the period of the group meetings. You can devote a short period on the strong average scores, or devote all your available time to the more problematic outcomes. Some group leaders have even decided to spend a session on each of the thirty-five outcomes, while others who have only a limited time as a group together have decided to spend one session on every one of the Five Dimensions. These are all valuable strategies that can be determined by the group and the time commitment they have given to you.

6. At the first session, members should bring their confidential assessment with them and participate in the discussions as they pursue their road to healthy discipleship.

7. With the presentation of every outcome, the group should spend time investigating the Scriptures, and discuss how their score on this outcome impacts their Christian witness in their world. We also have developed a list of books and resources on the Five Dimensions that we feel can assist in this journey.

8. Between your sessions, you can give the group members homework to read, study, and meditate on the identified outcome until they can understand how they need to discipline themselves to achieve that outcome in their daily life.

9. You can progress from one outcome to another as fast as the context and the time commitment of the group allows you to deal with more outcomes.

10. After a period of growth and development, you can ask the group to return to the website and take the free, re-assessment. The re-assessment will display the new scores on your dashboard and compare them with the ones of the initial assessment. At this point, you may find that some other scores are now in need of attention, and that your group has a new set of strong points. Discipleship is a dynamic process that requires us to constantly adapt our responses to changing life circumstances. This is how you can help the body of Christ to show what "walking in the Spirit" (Gal 5:16) is actually all about!

VOCATIONS AND OCCUPATIONS:
Clarity on Callings and Jobs

Dr. Charlie Self

Our Work and the Common Good

We have rich resources being produced by many wonderful practitioners and scholars on faith and work, economics and ethics, and flourishing churches and communities that can help us be whole and extend this vision of wholeness to others.

Amid all this fruitful work, the words, "vocation" and "vocational" and the synonymous terms "calling" "mission" and "purpose" are woven into the narratives and principles shared with God's people. "Vocation(al)" is the most used in the recent literature, and its meanings are expansive and sometimes unclear. *The aim of this essay is clarity on the term vocation and its relationship with occupation. Put another way, God's people need biblical clarity and insight on integrating their vocations (callings) and their occupations (everyday work).* These two terms are connected but not synonymous.

Vocation in History and Twenty-First-Century Expression

The term "vocation" comes from the Latin, *vocare*—to call or receive a call. For almost two millennia in Christian-influenced communities and cultures, vocation referred to a religious calling: a monastic order, missionary work, or parish labor. During the medieval era, vocation expanded beyond the clerical and embraced medicine (the doctor), law (the attorney) and teaching (the professor/teacher). Other occupations were respected, but not given the same status.

The Reformation rekindled the idea of the priesthood of all believers (Exod 19; 1 Pet 2) and began the practice of honoring everyday work as a calling from God. Martin Luther's delightful observation that Christian shoemaking is not about adding crosses to shoes but making good shoes was a breakthrough for workers in all classes. Alas, the potential of gospel liberation was often stymied by ungodly divisions and stereotypes of class, gender, and race. And the clerical vocation (that of pastors, teachers, missionaries, and other church workers) continued being placed above the others.

In the past century, the present work of the Holy Spirit in empowering believers for God's mission has resulted in unprecedented growth of global Christianity and—in wonderful moments of grace—greater cooperation among gospel-centered movements.

In most gospel-centered communities, we are seeing better elevation and empowerment of all believers, without despising the important callings of those set apart by Christ to nourish the Body and make Him known locally and globally (Eph 4). The term "vocation" is being muddied and overused in our zeal for encouraging missional living by our church members.

Toward Clarity: Understanding Our Vocation(s)

With this context in mind, let's define vocation and occupation—each in one sentence.

Vocation(s): General and specific callings from God that edify the Body, enhance the world, and integrate with daily work while transcending current occupational assignments.

Occupation(s): Everyday labor for the glory of God and good of others that expresses our vocation(s) while not itself being the full expression of our callings.

A key text for integration is Colossians 3:17-24 which says that whatever our current role in the family or society, let us do all for the glory of God as a servant of Christ.

All believers have three or four vocational facets (or "lanes" of the one great calling)[38]—callings from God that supersede job descriptions, class, gender, race or national identity.

The first and greatest vocational facet is God's calling to enter a relationship with the triune Lord through Jesus Christ. This is the "general calling" to repentance and faith

---

38 Os Guinness, *The Call: Anniversary Edition* (Nashville: Thomas Nelson, 2018), ii-xi.

(Acts 2-3, Rom 10) unto salvation, with Spirit-infused faith, hope, and love engendering security about identity and destiny (Rom 5-8). Obedience to this vocation begins with the Great Commandment of Jesus to love God with all our being, and love our neighbors unselfishly as ourselves (Matt 22; John 13-17). This vocation, our "first love" (Rev 2), is also demonstrated in obedience to the Great Commission as God's people share their faith across the street and around the world (Matt 28:18-20; Acts 1:8).

The second vocational facet consists of discovering and doing the "good works" designed by Jesus Christ for each believer (Eph 2:8-10; 3:3-10; 4:1-16). These works include our daily tasks but are more than job assignments. They include discovering and expressing our gifts (Rom 12; 1 Cor 12-14; Eph 4; 1 Tim 2) and wisely investing the resources our Lord has entrusted to us (Matt 25). Some of these good works are found within Christian gatherings. Others are expressed in and through the public and private work done all day. Here is where integration of vocation and occupation occur. I may be called as an elder and teacher in my church. My daily job as a customer service manager will allow me to use my vocational gifts for the business while not allowing the business to define my life. Conversely, I am no less an elder, pastor, apostle, or prophet if I sustain myself and my family with daily labor outside the largesse of the local church!

The third vocational facet is our calling to marriage or singleness. This may be seasonal or for a lifetime. The family is the first vital unit of a flourishing economy. Single women and men have advantages and challenges in their estate

(1 Cor 7), and married spouses must sacrifice for each other's good (Eph 5:22-33). Singleness is not incompleteness, and marriage is not the answer to all needs! The biological family designed by the Creator is the norm for most. Today, this norm is now questioned, rejected, and scorned by many, regardless of countless studies and biblical affirmation. For believers, marriage and family constitute a true vocation.

A fourth area of vocation: God calls His people to specific domains that are part of His providential ordering of society, from labor to leadership, intellectual and cultural domains, and all sorts of jobs. We should never rain on the parade of a believer excited about any kind of daily work! What we can do is expand their sense of calling while affirming the goodness of their daily work.

The guiding idea here is that God calls (*vocare*) people to influence and leadership is these areas. People may discover this calling accidentally, or they may deliberately learn about their field(s) of impact for God's Kingdom. There is no unimportant work—only particular assignments. For example, there are people gifted with concrete artisan abilities, others with abstract intellectual gifts, and many with various combinations of desires and abilities. Shaping personal and family mission around God-given capacities (which can grow) and dreams makes life richer and more adaptable.

In sum, believers have four vocations or callings (or facets/lanes of vocation), even as (demonstrated below) they work at many occupations:

- Called to Christ and His Kingdom and mission—making disciples and joining God in the restoration of all things

- Called to specific good works designed by God for the Church and society

- If single, called to celibate devotion to the Kingdom and completeness in Christ; if married, called to family fidelity; and if with children, called to nurture the next generation

- Called to specific domains of influence for God's glory and the good of the world

The above order is not placing work over family; nor is it placing ministry over care for spouse or children. It is movement from general/universal vocations to more particular ones. These are not a list of priorities but facets of a beautiful life God has designed.

Toward Clarity:
The Goodness of All (Moral) Occupations

Believers fulfill all their vocations as they work and participate in the economy.

Defining work and the economy:

- *Work is all moral and meaningful activity apart from leisure and rest.* It includes paid and unpaid activity, labor and leadership, creative and repetitious activity. Work is a primary expression of neighborly love and the context for extending God's mission.

- *Economies are moral and social systems of exchange, locally and globally.*

It is important that a biblical worldview inform how we see economics and work. The extremes of individualism and collectivism are always waiting to destroy agency or undermine unselfish community.

The creation mandates of Genesis 1-2 and the fulfillment of God's purposes in Revelation 19-22 include humankind engaged in meaningful work. For some believers, it comes as a shock to realize that our reward for good work in this life is more work in the next (Matt 25)!

Work is a primary expression of neighborly love and the context for extending God's mission. Occupations are also as fulfilling as the person's personality, giftedness, education, and acquired skills. We often forget that Jesus and the apostles addressed people who had fewer choices than we enjoy. In fact, for most of history, most people have not had choices about their economic status/work, their spouse, or their geography! And yet, the gospel was spread through these ordinary folks.

Occupations change based on the local and global economy and the context of culture, geography, and history. Our identity and vocation are greater than current employment. Occupations are also as fulfilling as the person's personality, giftedness, education, and acquired skills. In the twenty-first century, believers must awaken to their God-given callings and discover how they should be expressed in a rapidly changing world.

In the twenty-first century, believers must awaken to

their God-given callings and discover how they should be expressed in a rapidly changing world. Jobs that now employ millions will not exist in a few years (i.e., a traditional auto mechanic). Conversely, many jobs yet unconceived of or only in their infancy (new technologies, information systems, and innovative manufacturing) will employ multitudes. Regardless of these changes, God's vocations of relationship in Christ, good works reflecting divine appointments and social impact, and family fidelity will remain until the end of time.

Occupations involve competencies that include both natural abilities and acquired skills; spiritual gifts are often a delightful part of the process as well, especially discernment, word of wisdom, faith, and word of knowledge. In our discipleship processes, we must help followers of Jesus grow in the unchanging ways of the Lord while gaining the knowledge, skills, and wisdom for employment in an ever-evolving economy.

Three Enduring Principles Concerning Our Occupations and Workplace Presence

Godly character is primary in all aspect of work. All good work is done for God's glory and the good of others, with full integrity. Creativity, peacemaking, and servanthood should guide all daily work. Giftedness and growing competencies do matter, but the fruit of the Spirit as well as cardinal Christian virtues are foundational.

The Church operates under a new Kingdom sociology (Gal 3:28-4:7). All God's people enjoy equality before the Lord, in fellowship around the Table, and in access to all God-ordained assignments. Economic class, ethnic identity, gender, or religious background do not determine divine assignments. Philemon's runaway slave Onesimus, led to Christ by the Apostle Paul, was both restored in fellowship and later made a bishop! Alas, our workaday environments do not always reflect these values.

We work in a fallen-and being-redeemed world and must confront both individual iniquity and institutional injustice[39] as we labor for the Lord. When St. Paul exhorted slaves to serve their master, Jesus Christ, with good conscience and also exhorted masters to remember that they are slaves to Christ, he fostered the conditions for ending slavery and restoring dignity to all people. We have a divine obligation to "do justice" (Mic 6:8) and "break the yoke" of oppression (Isa 58) so all people can flourish.

Practically, most of humankind does not go to work whistling a cheery tune and excited about their place in the economy! This can change with better teaching on vocation and the dignity of all good work; however, *change can also include serious efforts for better pay and working conditions, access to markets, the rule of law and property rights that open opportunities for all to prosper.*

---

[39] Chris Brooks, "Rethinking Urban Poverty: Context, Data, and Collaboration," talk delivered for Oikonomia Network, Economic Wisdom, accessed June 28, 2022, https://economicwisdom.org/2020/03/27/christopher-brooks-rethinking-urban-poverty-context-data-and-collaboration/.

Perspective Matters: A Call to Maturity

Throughout most of history, people of all cultures and geographies have spent their days locked in a system, with few choices concerning work, marriage, and geography. Over time and through globalization, more options for more people are creating conditions for flourishing—as well as causing unsettling expectations as workers realize that the job they prepared for may not exist tomorrow.

It is encouraging to see exponential reductions in abject poverty and encouraging that more churches are seeing their mission as whole-life discipleship that connects Sunday worship and Monday work while integrating business and charitable activity. It is encouraging that there is an awakening to God's vocations and more people discovering their gifts and callings.

For pastors and all who equip the saints for their works of service (inside and outside the church), these ideas on vocation and occupation serve as a clarion call to clear thinking, careful articulation, and detailed planning for effective discipleship. Beginning with the infusion of a joyful work ethic with children all the way to strategic deployment of retirees in service of the church and society, the Church needs clarity of language, focus on (character and community) outcomes, alignment with Kingdom values, and momentum of the Holy Spirit.

A Final Note

All these ideas boil down to believers realizing that they are more than their current jobs, and yet their current placement is a Kingdom opportunity. Learning daily contentment yoked with Jesus (Matt 11) while aspiring to the fullness of Christ and His vocation (Phil 3) is the paradoxical power of the gospel. Today's discipline is tomorrow's destiny—and a vision of vocation makes our current occupation meaningful.

Select Bibliography

The following websites and recommended books are just a small portion of excellent resources available as we reimagine discipleship, retool our organizations, and refresh our communities.

Here is the Discipleship dynamics Assessment (DDA)™ site: www.discipleshipdynamics.com.

Some websites that will be helpful for whole-life discipleship and faith-work integration

- o www.pathmakersfnd.org — Pathmakers Foundation: funding and walking with leaders transforming their communities one zip code at a time with new ideas, models, and collaborations
- o www.compact.family — Compact Family Services: mobilizing the church to reach the most vulnerable
- o www.madetoflourish.org — Helping pastors and local churches integrate faith, work, and economics wisdom for the flourishing of their communities
- o www.oikonomianetwork.org — Economic wisdom for church leaders
- o Some Seminary Faith and Work Centers:
    - o Gordon Conwell's Mockler Center
    - o https://www.gordonconwell.edu/center-for-workplace-ethics/
    - o Asbury's Office for Faith Work, and Economics https://asburyseminary.edu/resources/ofwe/
    - o The Assemblies of God Theological Seminary's Center for Faith, Work, and Economics https://agts.edu/ministry-resources/faith-work-economics/

- Dallas Theological Seminary's Hendrick's Center (see Darrell Bock's Table Podcasts) https://hendrickscenter.dts.edu
- www.inst.net and www.repurposing.biz – Spirit-filled leadership and resources for Kingdom transformation
- www.tifwe.org – The Institute for Faith, Work, and Economics
- www.davidgill.org – David Gill is one of the pioneers of the contemporary and diverse faith and work movement
- www.acton.org – Co-founded by Kris Mauren and Father Robert Sirico, Acton exists to unite good intentions with sound economics and promote a free and virtuous society.
- www.theologyofwork.org — Wil Messenger leads a creative team curating biblical resources for empowering all vocations and occupations
- www.faithdrivenentreprenuer.org – founded by Henry Kaestner: offers resources for business leaders and spiritual leaders
- www.renovare.org — founded by Richard Foster, author of *Celebration of Discipline* Renovare focuses on spiritual formation,
- www.cpjustice.org — Center for Public Justice: a great resource for public square wisdom
- www.chalmers.org — Chalmers Center at Covenant College: The leading Christian poverty alleviation organization, led by Brian Fikkert
- www.denverinstitute.org — Denver Institute for Faith and Work
- www.cpjustice.org — the Center for Public Justice is a Christian think tank dedicated to fostering wise public policies that are as inclusive as possible.

Bibliography

Some Books for Each of the Five Dimensions of Discipleship

For Spiritual Formation
(Loving God with All Our Being)

- St. Augustine, *Confessions*
- Thomas à Kempis, *The Imitation of Christ*
- Martin Luther, *The Freedom of the Christian*
- Andrew Arndt, *All Flame: Entering into the Life of the Father, Son and Holy Spirit*
- Richard Foster, *Celebration of Discipline and Streams of Living Water*
- Dallas Willard, *The Divine Conspiracy and The Spirit of the Disciplines*
- Cyd Holzclaw and Geoff Holzclaw, *Does God Really like Me?*
- Jack Hayford, *Prayer is Invading the Impossible*
- Gordon Fee and Doug Stuart, *How to Read the Bible for All Its Worth*
- Arthur Wallis, *God's Chosen Fast*

For Personal Wholeness

- Peter Scazzero, *The Emotionally Healthy Church and Emotionally Healthy Spirituality*
- Henry Cloud, *Changes that Heal*
- Louis Husser, *Forgiving Others: The Key to Healing Deep Wounds of Your Past*
- Jason Wilson, *Cry Like a Man*
- Stephen Arterburn, *Every Man's Battle*
- Shannon Ethridge, *Every Woman's Battle*

- Geri Scazzero, *The Emotionally Healthy Woman: Eight Things You Have to Quit to Change Your Life*
- Max Lucado, Unshakable Hope: *Building our Lives on the Promises of God*
- Tish Harrison Warren and Andy Crouch, *Liturgy of the Ordinary: Sacred Practices for Everyday Life.*

For Healthy Relationships

- John Perkins: *One Blood: Parting Words to the Church on Race and Love*
- Irwin Ince, *The Beautiful Community*
- Tara Beth Leach, *Radiant: Recovering the Witness of the Church*
- Gary Chapman, *The 5 Love Languages*
- Alan Loy McGinnis, *The Friendship Factor*
- Henry Cloud and John Townsend, *Boundaries*
- Craig Groeschel and Amy Groeschel, *From This Day Forward: Five Commitments to Fail Proof Your Marriage*
- Owen Strachan, ed., Whole in Christ: *A Biblical Approach to Singleness*

For Vocational Clarity

- Brett Johnson, *Convergence, Lemon Leadership, Transforming Society*
- Os Guinness, *The Call*
- Tim Keller, *Every Good Endeavor*
- Paige Wiley and Luke Bobo, *Worked Up: Navigating Calling After College*
- Don Fortune and Katie Fortune, *Discovering your God-Given Gifts*
- Joseph Castleberry, *Your Deepest Dream: Discovering*

God's True Vision for Your Life
- Gene Veith, *God at Work: Your Christian Vocation in All of Life*
- Steve Garber: *Visions of Vocation: Common Grace for the Common Good, The Seamless Life*
- Amy Sherman, *Kingdom Calling: Vocational Stewardship for the Common Good, and Agents of Flourishing: Pursuing Shalom in Every Corner of Society*
- A. J. Swoboda, *Tongues and Trees: A Pentecostal Eco-Theology*

For Economic Wisdom and Work

- Tom Nelson, *Work Matters, The Economics of Neighborly Love, The Flourishing Pastor*
- The Oikonomia Network, *A Vision of Flourishing Communities*
- Charlie Self, *Flourishing Churches and Communities*
- Luke Bobo, *Race, Apologetics, and Economics: Is There a Connection?*
- Svetlana Papazov, *Becoming a Church for Monday*
- Chuck Proudfit and Jeff Greer, *Biznistry*
- Brian Fikkert and Steve Corbett, *When Helping Hurts*
- Brian Fikkert, *Becoming Whole*
- Brian Rhodes, Robbie Holt, and Brian Fikkert, *Practicing the King's Economy*
- Ron Blue, *Master Your Money*

Life in 5D

www.ingramcontent.com/pod-product-compliance
Lightning Source LLC
Chambersburg PA
CBHW070140080526
44586CB00015B/1772